Review Comment Analysis for E-commerce

East China Normal University Scientific Reports
Subseries on Data Science and Engineering

ISSN: 2382-5715

Vol. 1 High-Frequency Trading and Probability Theory
by Zhaodong Wang (East China Normal University)
and Weian Zheng (East China Normal University)

Vol. 2 School Mathematics Textbooks in China:
Comparative Study and Beyond
by Jianpan Wang (East China Normal University)

Vol. 3 Querying and Mining Uncertain Data Streams
by Cheqing Jin (East China Normal University)
and Aoying Zhou (East China Normal University)

Vol. 4 Opinion Analysis for Online Reviews
by Yuming Lin (Guilin University of Electronic Technology, China),
Xiaoling Wang (East China Normal University, China) and
Aoying Zhou (East China Normal University, China)

Vol. 5 Review Comment Analysis for E-commerce
by Rong Zhang (East China Normal University, China),
Aoying Zhou (East China Normal University, China),
Wenzhe Yu (East China Normal University, China),
Yifan Gao (East China Normal University, China) and
Pingfu Chao (East China Normal University, China)

East China Normal University Scientific Reports | Vol. 5
Subseries on Data Science and Engineering

Review Comment Analysis for E-commerce

Rong Zhang
East China Normal University, China

Aoying Zhou
East China Normal University, China

Wenzhe Yu
East China Normal University, China

Yifan Gao
East China Normal University, China

Pingfu Chao
East China Normal University, China

NEW JERSEY • LONDON • SINGAPORE • BEIJING • SHANGHAI • HONG KONG • TAIPEI • CHENNAI • TOKYO

Published by

World Scientific Publishing Co. Pte. Ltd.

5 Toh Tuck Link, Singapore 596224

USA office: 27 Warren Street, Suite 401-402, Hackensack, NJ 07601

UK office: 57 Shelton Street, Covent Garden, London WC2H 9HE

Library of Congress Cataloging-in-Publication Data
Names: Zhang, Rong, Ph. D., author.
Title: Review comment analysis for e-commerce / Rong Zhang (East China Normal University, China), Aoying Zhou (East China Normal University, China), Wenzhe Yu (East China Normal University, China), Yifan Gao (East China Normal University, China) & Pingfu Chao (East China Normal University, China).
Description: New Jersey : World Scientific, 2016. | Series: East China Normal University scientific reports ; Volume 5 | Includes bibliographical references.
Identifiers: LCCN 2016013142 | ISBN 9789813100046 (hc : alk. paper) | ISBN 9789813100053 (pbk : alk. paper)
Subjects: LCSH: Electronic commerce.
Classification: LCC HF5548.32 .Z43 2016 | DDC 658.8/72--dc23
LC record available at https://lccn.loc.gov/2016013142

British Library Cataloguing-in-Publication Data
A catalogue record for this book is available from the British Library.

Desk Editor: Herbert Moses

Typeset by Stallion Press
Email: enquiries@stallionpress.com

Printed in Singapore

East China Normal University Scientific Reports

Preface

Web 2.0 provides users an opportunity to publish useful information for others. One of the representative application scenarios is product comment platform. The platform allows the user of a product or service to write reviews including a description and an overall evaluation score. Generally, the description is not of many words and the evaluation score is between 1 and 5 in the format of stars. Such kind of user-generated content is exploding and brings new opportunities for product organization, recommendation, user profiling, and so on. However, with increasing data, efficient usage to this kind of data has become a problem due to the increase in both volume and variety.

Volume and variety bring difficulty in information organization, i.e., the organization of a large set of unstructured data. Information organization aims at presenting or demonstrating the most useful information hidden behind textual information. Additionally, the increase in products without the uniform schema definition makes product filtering difficult while searching. For the allurement of economical benefit, noisy or fake information may broadly appear inside those information; to know difference in expertise for diverse categories, user reviews may have the problem of credibility, which have been taken equally in the current evaluation system. Comment description generally presents much more information than numerical rating, which includes multifaceted opinions for variety aspects. This information can enrich either user or product profile for better recommendation performance. In this book, the following issues are addressed considering the better usage of review comment:

- *Customer Credibility Learning.* We design a twin-bipartite-graph modeling the shopping and reviewing behaviors between shops, customers and products. This work defines the credibility as to what extent review content or rating can be believed in, which is a big extension to traditional spammer detection. It analyzes the difference between individual review behaviors and the group of other customers, and designs a novel feedback mechanism to adjust individual credibility.
- *Entity Resolution.* Traditional entity resolution methods perform well on structured data. As noise increases in description, it has an obvious decline in performance. We propose to combine structured data and unstructured data together for production normalization. One method is for centralized processing. It employs schema integration and value confirmation, which reinforce each other. The other method is for distributed processing. It transforms high dimensional product vectors into low dimensional signatures by using locality sensitive hash. It can improve matching performance by random permutations. Finally, it is implemented on MapReduce framework.
- *TopK Review Selection.* Providing users with a concise set of topK representative reviews is one of the methods for review organization. We provide a new method for topK set generation. Our method focuses not only on aspect coverage and opinion diversity, but also on aspect importance. It is proved to be more applicable.
- *Review Summarization.* Generating summarization from the large set of review content is defined to extract a small size of description snippets for each product. Each snippet is composed of a product, the surround description context with obvious opinions and a numerical score. We design two types of summarization methods. The first one employs a hierarchical tree to classify description term semantically. Representative snippets are selected with respect to both opinion and aspect distributions. The second one designs a new bilateral topic model, incorporating aspect and score as two independent dimensions. A joint algorithm is proposed for snippet selection.
- *Recommendation.* We present a novel recommendation algorithm which explores the connections between numerical ratings and review content.

It employs a topic model on review text to find the hidden topics and the review distribution on each topic. Users and products are profiled based on these hidden topics. Linear or Logistic regression model is applied to gain the relationship between ratings and topic distributions. User or product profiles are fed into the learned model for rating prediction.

Rong Zhang, Aoying Zhou, Wenzhe Yu, Yifan Gao, Pingfu Chao

Shanghai, China
April, 2015

Acknowledgments

This research was supported by National High Technology Research and Development Program of China (863 Program) (No. 2012AA011003) and the National Science Foundation of China (Nos. 61103039, 61232002, 61402180 and 61402177).

We thank all friends, Zhenjie Zhang, Xiaoyan Yang, XiaoFeng He and Ming Gao, without whom the technical contributions of this book cannot be worked out.

We would like to express our sincere thanks and appreciation to the people at the University Press, for their generous help throughout the publication preparation process.

Contents

Chapter 1

Introduction

1.1 Background

Web 2.0 sites allow users to do more than just retrieving information. Instead of merely reading, users are encouraged to comment on published articles, update their status in social networking sites (SNS), and collaborate by editing questions in question-and-answer sites. User-generated content (UGC) is now part of the online experience to billions of Internet users worldwide.

As online shopping grows, E-commerce is expanding internationally. In E-commerce sites, one of the major UGC is review information, which consists of consumers' purchase history, ratings and reviews, product description provided by merchants, and friendships between users. Moreover, the popularity of mobile devices produces a large amount of location-based data. For example, users can check in restaurants, shops and other places of interest by mobile applications, and share their locations and likes with friends. According to the about page,[1] Taobao.com, the most popular consumer-to-consumer (C2C) platform in China, has about 500 million registered users, with more than 60 million visitors everyday. It sells 48,000 products per minute out of the total 800 million provided per day. On the other hand, Yelp.com, a crowd-sourced local business review site, hosts 67 million reviews,[2] while Dianping.com, a Chinese version of Yelp, gets 60 million reviews,[3] as shown in their websites.

[1] http://www.taobao.com/about/intro.php
[2] http://www.yelp.com/about
[3] http://www.dianping.com/aboutus

The growth in users, products, as well as trading volume brings huge UGC in E-commerce sites, and yields heterogeneous or unstructured data from various sources. Among different types of UGC, online reviews, especially the rating or score[4] and a piece of descriptive text, have a great impact on both consumers and merchants. Consumers comment on products they bought, in the aspects of quality, service, delivery, etc. Potential buyers can read reviews, in addition to seller's description, to get a clear picture of a certain product. This helps to judge products and make purchase decision based on other people's shopping experience. Furthermore, these reviews may reveal user preference, which can serve as feedback to merchants to improve their service and recommend products to target users.

However, the properties of noise, heterogeneity and sheer size prevent the efficient usage of online reviews. In this book, we focus on solving the problems introduced by these properties, including reviewer quality assessment, product normalization, review organization and recommendation application.

1.2 Challenges

People experience product searching and viewing in online shopping. They choose products with high scores, and compare similar products from different merchants. They can get further information on products by reading reviews from other consumers. As reviews are generated without a strict/predefined control, they are noisy; as reviews are produced by different applications, especially the moving terminal, it does not have the uniform schema and is expanding faster and faster. In order to make the usage of reviews easy and efficient, several techniques are employed. We learn user credibility to rank products fairly, and apply entity resolution to classify similar products, which enhances the product lists presented to users. We select or summarize product reviews for easy information browsing. In addition, personalized recommendations are made supplementary to the product list.

---

[4]We use the word rating and score interchangeably in this book to denote the numeric value assigned to a product which reflects user satisfaction on this product.

Credibility Learning. When shopping online, people first search for products they want by keywords. A list of products ranked by overall scores is returned to users for comparison. Generally, a product's overall score is calculated by averaging all the review scores it has received. People usually click on the top few products to get more information. However, driven by the economic benefits, there exist noisy data, e.g., undeserving high scores for product promotion or false low scores to damage competitors' reputation, which results in inaccurate evaluation. In an extreme case of our work, review spammers intentionally give fake reviews and ratings. Moreover, as the reviews grow in E-commerce sites, manually reading to judge review reliability is not feasible. Hence, it is crucial to learn the credibility of reviewers to re-score and rank products/ratings fairly.

As we survey, the following two observations may cause the noisy data in product scoring: (1) some customers do not give out fair reviews; (2) there is inconsistency between the score and the comment of a review. For the first observation, it is due to the fake rating mentioned above or the user behavior characteristics such as giving gentle evaluation. For the second observation, the inconsistency means that a review consists of a high score and a negative comment. This happens because of the two reasons: One is that though giving high scores, consumers may write some disadvantages which do not affect their shopping experience; the other one is because of the pressure from merchants who want to have more high scores by the so called after-sell services, if you assign low scores. Considering these two observation, it is necessary to analyze user review behaviors for user credibility.

We design an approach to tackle the above problems and calculate the new overall scores for products by two steps. The first step is to employ a supervised learning method to correct the inconsistency between review scores and comments. Newly autopredicted scores are then used as customers' review scores for calculating the overall scores. The second step is to evaluate user credibility, so that the originally assigned ratings of products and shops are then adjusted according to it. We construct a twin-bipartite graph to model the review relationship among users, products and shops, which is not fully exploited in previous work. We design a novel feedback strategy to increase and decrease user credibility iteratively over the graph by comparing individual ratings with collective ratings. Our basic idea behind is: good products deserve high review scores while bad products should be given low scores; good customers should assign high scores to good products and low scores to bad products.

Entity Resolution. The rapid growth in both variety and quantity of products sold online brings difficulty in product organization, which may also affect user experience. Products without uniform schema and strict description specification may lead to search results either too few or too much. When searching for a product by keywords, customers would be disappointed with the duplicate products in a diversified result list. And sometimes they want to compare a group of similar products from various merchants, so search results containing products quite different from each other may not be satisfying. Hence, it is critical to apply entity resolution, which identifies instances that represent the same real-world entity, for products in E-commerce sites to further enhance the product list. Moreover, user-generated product descriptions may introduce intended errors for economic purpose; or there are vacant values on the descriptions. Mining the unstructured review text to help normalize products will be important for product organization.

We design two entity resolution frameworks, which are centralized and distributed respectively, to find products or records that refer to the same entity. We first introduce the centralized one, which achieves product normalization by schema integration and data cleaning. A graph-based method is proposed for schema integration to produce uniform and meaningful representation of products. Then we conduct data cleaning to create precise and comprehensive description for each product. The evidence extracted from textual information is utilized for data cleaning, including missing value filling, incorrect value correction and value confirmation. Finally, we distinguish products by clustering on product similarity matrix learned from logistic regression.

However, entity resolution is a compute-intensive job as it needs to compare each pair of records, thus the complexity of traditional matching algorithms is not feasible for large datasets. To handle the massive property of products in E-commerce sites, we design a distributed entity resolution framework and implement a fast matching algorithm based on MapReduce. MapReduce, a distributed computing framework, is well suited for entity matching as the pairwise similarity computation can be executed in parallel. Based on the unstructured product description data, we can generate high dimensional vectors for products. However, high dimension may cause dimensional curse when doing similarity calculating. We propose to transform the high dimensional vectors to lower dimensional signatures by a specified locality sensitive hash (LSH) function. We introduce a bunch of random algorithms to do signature permutation ensuring that similar products will be matched in a high probability. In order to reduce redundant computation which is a pervasive problem for entity resolution on MapReduce, we design our own algorithm to remove redundancy. Our designed entity matching framework exhibits good capabilities in promising load balancing and lowering network transmission.

Review Selection. It is common for people to click on products in the ranking list and read reviews to get product details for decision-making. However, as online reviews proliferate in recent years, E-commerce sites are facing the problem of information overload. On the one hand, it is too time-consuming for users to go through all the reviews for a certain product, especially for those popular and trending items. On the other hand, an increasing number of users choose to shop via mobile devices. Due to the limitation of screen size, these users prefer to read a small fraction of reviews to make their purchase decision in a short time. To support such kind of applications, it is necessary and urgent to select a subset of reviews that covers useful information for each product and presented to users for reference.

E-commerce sites have adopted several representative review selection methods based on review ranking. Review ranking ranks reviews according to their helpfulness votes, so as to provide top-k reviews to users. Helpfulness votes are evaluated by users to those reviews that are helpful to them. And there are also a number of researches on automatically estimating the quality of reviews [Kim *et al.* (2006); Liu *et al.* (2007); Tsur and Rappoport (2009); Hong *et al.* (2012)], but they have two drawbacks as follows. First, the resulting top-k reviews of a product may contain redundant information while some important attributes may not be covered. Second, since previous experiments [Danescu-Niculescu-Mizil *et al.* (2009)] show that users tend to consider helpful for the reviews that follow the mainstream, the resulting top-*k* reviews may lack opinion diversity. By these two observations, review selection based on attribute coverage [Tsaparas *et al.* (2011)] is proposed. It prefers to choose reviews covering as many attributes as possible, which does not reflect the original opinion distribution. Then Lappas *et al.* (2012) proposed selecting a set of reviews that keeps the proportion of positive and negative opinions on each attribute. But we have found that this work does not perform well especially for selecting a few reviews, which is caused by the overlooking of attribute importance.

Hence, to improve the overall value of the top-*k* reviews, we view the top-*k* reviews as a review set rather than simple aggregation of reviews. We propose an approach to select a small set of high quality reviews that cover important attributes and diversified opinions. A Support Vector Machine (SVM) regression function is learned from both textual and user preference features to estimate review quality. We also evaluate the importance of attributes by calculating their weights. In order to improve the diversity of the resulting top-*k* reviews, we cluster reviews into different topic groups, and select reviews proportionally from each group to preserve opinion distribution.

Review Summarization. Instead of representative review selection, review summarization is to sketch the overall opinion among different aspects hidden in reviews. Previous work normally acts on the assumption that each individual review has one discussion object. For example, a book review is about a particular book. However, there are reviews with different discussion objects, such as restaurants and trip reviews. User-generated reviews for a restaurant are different from those for a single product, as a restaurant review is generally a mixture of opinions on various dishes. People concern about the food, service and environment of restaurants. In particular, they are keen to know the taste, quality and component of each dish, as they can only try a few dishes once. Though previous works have made review summaries on different aspects, they do not consider the latent semantic relationships among them. Thus, the conciseness of summaries is reduced. This results in a brand new review summarization task that extracts information for each dish from the reviews of a certain restaurant. Moreover, there is only one overall rating assigned to a dining experience, leading to the difficulties in gaining viewpoints on each dish.

To complete the new task, we try to generate product-oriented or dish-oriented summaries,[5] each of which consists of an evaluation score and key comments on a product which contain common opinions from past customers. Furthermore, as a piece of summary should be concise enough to fit into the screens of mobile devices, we partition the comments into short snippets to provide a small set of representative snippets. Therefore, our new task includes two subtasks for summarizing the reviews of a product: (1) estimate the product score which is different from the restaurant's overall score; (2) select descriptive snippets that can well represent the comments on the product.

We provide two solutions to product-oriented review summarization. The first solution employs a hierarchical term tree to classify terms semantically. It considers two aspects: opinion-aspects which refer to the positive or negative opinions on products, and attribute-aspects which refer to the description of product features. This solution has three steps: (1) extract product snippets; (2) predict snippet scores; (3) summarize product snippets. In the first step, we extract the surrounding words of products as snippets and classify whether the snippets contain opinions. In the second step, we predict the opinion scores of evaluative snippets using several different approaches. After the first two steps, we have the candidate snippets with predicted scores for each product. Then we could select snippets with respect to the opinion and attribute-aspects.

The second solution proposes a new bilateral topic model to support efficient and accurate analysis on review comments from the rating aspect and the text aspect. As an extension of latent Dirichlet allocation (LDA) [Blei *et al.* (2003)], our new model features a two-dimensional topic matrix, which incorporates aspects of dishes on one dimension and scores on the other. Every pair of aspect and score forms an individual topic, while at the same time the topic-dependent and score-dependent correlations are preserved in the topic matrix. We also derive a new inference algorithm

[5]The word product and dish are used interchangeably in review summarization.

for the model that can automatically extract labels of every word in the comments with probabilities on the aspect-score pairs. After model training, a joint algorithm is designed for snippet selection, which exploits the probabilistic information on the possible aspects and scores of snippets on dishes.

Recommendation. So far, there are two major approaches to produce recommendations [Rajaraman and Ullman (2012)]: content-based filtering and collaborative filtering. They typically rely on analyzing users' past rating behavior to make predictions on new items for a user, in which unstructured review text is not utilized. However, the sheer review text contains abundant information about users' opinions and preferences, which are valuable to any recommendation system. Therefore, we study the application of review comments in recommender systems.

There has been ample work [Popescu and Etzioni (2005); Pang and Lee (2008); Titov and McDonald (2008a, 2008b); Brody and Elhadad (2010); Jo and Oh (2011)] on review analysis from aspect discovery, sentiment analysis to opinion mining, but none of them studies the linkage between ratings and review text for product recommendation. Though some model is designed for predicting the rating of a given review, they cannot be directly applied to a recommender system in that the user–item relationship is not captured. The work most related to ours is explained by McAuley and Leskovec (2013), in which Hidden Factors as Topics (HFT) is proposed to combine ratings with review text for product recommendation. HFT aligns hidden factors in ratings with hidden topics in reviews to create user/item profiles, which are then fit into SVD to make rating predictions. The problem with HFT is that each time the review text is associated with one of the two dimensions, i.e., either from items' perspective or from users' perspective, which means the hidden topics discovered only reflect the hidden factors of ratings from one dimension.

We present a recommendation algorithm that novelly explores the connections between ratings and review text. We employ a topic model on review text to find hidden topics and the review distribution on each topic. In particular, we utilize the topics and their distributions to model users and products in a common latent space. Our rating prediction model is then built on linear/logistic regression to gain the relationship between ratings and topic distributions. The combination of user/product profiles is fed into the learned model to predict ratings.

1.3 Related Work

Since the UGC-based analysis and application in E-commerce sites are related to credibility learning, entity resolution, review selection and summarization, as well as recommendation, we conclude the existing work in these areas in this section.

Credibility Learning. Trustworthiness modeling is extensively exploited in E-commerce sites. Active work has been done to develop incentive mechanisms to encourage honesty, including side payment mechanisms [Miller *et al.* (2005); Jurca and Faltings (2003)] and credibility mechanisms [Papaioannou and Stamoulis (2005); Jurca and Faltings (2004)]. Side payment mechanisms reward customers with fair ratings to the service offers. Thus providing fair ratings for business is a Nash equilibrium. Credibility mechanisms rely on the comparison among participants. If the ratings are different, credibility would be decreased. Since credibility is made public, it does affect business to a great extent. So, reviewers are encouraged to give fair ratings for their credibility.

The approaches on credibility analysis can be grouped into the following two types:

(1) Review content based: To evaluate review quality by different properties and rank these reviews. The explosion of UGC brings great efforts in content-based analysis. The main task is to design a set of algorithms to retrieve useful and reliable information for customers. Most of the previous works [Ghose and Ipeirotis (2010); Kim *et al.* (2006); Liu *et al.* (2007, 2008); Tsur and Rappoport (2009); Zhang and Varadarajan (2006); Morinaga *et al.* (2002)] emphasize on analyzing features in review content for detecting helpful reviews. This main purpose is to evaluate and select some useful reviews to read as described by Liu *et al.* (2007, 2008). Review quality is calculated by classification or regression model based on review content and tested on customers' voting data which act as the ground-truth. But the credibility of these ground-truth has never been studied. The widely used content features are *lexical*, *grammatical*, *semantic*, as well

as the *stylistic* levels. These characteristics are used to train a model to capture review quality. Zhang and Varadarajan (2006), Liu *et al.* (2007) and Tsur and Rappoport (2009) have verified that the syntactic features from the review content are most useful. Kim *et al.* (2006) use both content features and metadata features such as ratings, and find that ratings are most useful for their SVM regression model. Liu *et al.* (2008) take a nonlinear regression model to calculate helpfulness of reviews by inputting reviewer's expertise and timeline features. Morinaga *et al.* (2002) compare reviews of different products in one category to gain reputation of the target product by generating syntactic and linguistic rules in advance to determine the positive/negative opinions. It calculates the product reputation based on the reviews gathered from web search engines. Then it does summarization and classification to these reviews. Hu and Liu (2004) suggest to mine and summarize customers' reviews by different properties so as to ease browsing and checking activities. Lu *et al.* (2010) proposed the first work to exploit users social context information from voting relationship to predict review quality. The more positive votes a review gets, the better quality it has. All of these works have overlooked the quality of peers. Exploiting social context for review quality prediction was shown by Lu *et al.* (2010) by incorporating text-based quality prediction with four kinds of social context hypothesis separately.

(2) Reviewer based: To detect the quality of reviewers and filter reviews from low quality reviewers. Message source characteristics are found to influence judgment and behavior as shown by Ghose and Ipeirotis (2010), Chaiken (1980) and Brown and Reingen (1987). It is proved that product sales will be affected by reviewers' disclosure of identity-related information [Forman *et al.* (2008)]. But this work focuses on the disclosure of identity information, such as review history, its locality and ability in reviewing. They do not distinguish customers by their honesty. Customer credibility detection is exploited by Mizzaro (2003), Laureti *et al.* (2006), Yu *et al.* (2006), Zhou *et al.* (2011), Medo and Wakeling (2010), Li *et al.* (2012, 2014a) and Jindal and Liu (2008). Generally, a customer's credibility is determined by the aggregated difference between users' ratings and the item's ratings. They make use of users' credibility as the weight to eliminate the influence of bad ratings. These algorithms iteratively refine users' credibility scores and items' rating scores. Among these, spammer

detection [Jindal and Liu (2008); Zhou *et al.* (2011); Mukherjee *et al.* (2013a)] is a special case of credibility calculation, which divides the customers into two separate groups as spammers and non-spammers with credibility value setting to 0 and 1, respectively. But spammer detection cannot solve all the problems as we have listed before. So individual credibility is worth exploring. But existing work for credibility calculation as explained by Mizzaro (2003), Laureti *et al.* (2006), Yu *et al.* (2006) and Zhou *et al.* (2011) cannot guarantee the convergence and is hard to use. The ones similar to our work are explained by Li *et al.* (2012, 2014a). They calculate customer credibility relying on the difference between overall ratings and individual ratings, but these works take the difference equally to the credibility updating. Another form to evaluate customers' credibility is finding experts which is contrary to spammer detection as given by Zhu *et al.* (2013) and Balog *et al.* (2009). They focus on finding experts from the candidate set. Balog *et al.* (2009) propose a language modeling framework to find experts based on probability distribution and proof the convergence. Zhu *et al.* (2013) exploit both content-based category similarity and user interaction-based category similarity to accurately measure category relevancies. They combine an extended category link graph and a topical link analysis approach to find experts in a knowledge domain.

Danescu-Niculescu-Mizil *et al.* (2009) declared that not only review content but also related reviews are useful for review analysis. In this work, we absorb their observations and suggest to evaluate reviews by combining review content with its related context, including related reviews to products, customers and shops. Our work designs a novel feedback strategy considering the rating inconsistency, and we are the first to tackle the inconsistency between the semantic review content and the numerical review ratings. Our work is a complementary work to most of the previous work.

Entity Resolution. The idea of entity resolution, along with product normalization and entity matching, was first proposed by Newcombe *et al.* (1959). The traditional approach to entity resolution considers similarity of text. There has been extensive work on approximate string similarity measures [Monge *et al.* (1996); Navarro (2001); Chaudhuri *et al.*

(2003)] used in unsupervised entity resolution. They always have good performances on processing speed but lack high accuracies.

Machine learning approaches are introduced to improve the accuracy by learning string similarity measures from labeled data [Bilenko and Mooney (2003); Tejada *et al.* (2002); Sven Ristad and Yianilos (1998); Ananthakrishna *et al.* (2002)]. There have been some methods that enhance the traditional techniques by utilizing certain types of context entity reference to improve the quality [Ananthakrishna *et al.* (2002); Dong *et al.* (2005)]. The groundwork for posing entity resolution as a probabilistic classification problem was done by Fellegi and Sunter (1969). This was followed by Ravikumar and Cohen (2004) and Winkler (2002). Some recent works leverage knowledge acquired from external sources, such as Wikipedia and WorldNet, for domain-independent entity resolution [Cucerzan (2007); Bunescu and Pasca (2006)]. Some employ negative evidence for entity resolution [Dong *et al.* (2005); Whang *et al.* (2009); Lee *et al.* (2011)], which does not need every entity to have corresponding external resource. In the E-commerce domain, [Bilenko *et al.* (2005); Kannan *et al.* (2011)] proposed methods for clustering merchant offers, which is similar to our work. However, their work did not take noise into consideration and the similarity measures they used are sensitive to noise. As a result, the accuracy and recall of this method are low when the data is noisy.

Another part of work focuses on boosting the processing speed. At the end of 20th century, with the rapid growth in data size, the main problem for entity matching changed from improving calculation accuracy to handling huge amount of data. Blocking strategy was introduced to solve this problem for it can filter the majority of entity pairs with low similarity before similarity comparison. Meanwhile, since the limited performance of a single computer had become the bottleneck, the proposal of MapReduce [Dean and Ghemawat (2008)] based on distributed system also gave us a better platform to solve this problem. A number of blocking-based entity matching algorithms under MapReduce framework have been presented to help deal with big datasets [Kiefer *et al.* (2010); Kim and Shim (2012); Vernica *et al.* (2010); Lu *et al.* (2012)]. These works are based on the assumption that there is only one key for an entity and use a map/reduce phase to handle the problem. They design different blocking strategies for map phase and then do the matching step in reduce phase. Some of the most influential works include sorted neighborhood [Kolb *et al.* (2012c)] and load-balanced entity matching [Kolb *et al.* (2012a, 2012b)]. However, this part of the work and its joint work [Kolb *et al.* (2010)] did not mention the load balancing problem on MapReduce. On the other hand, both *BlockSplit* and *PairRange* blocking strategies mentioned in [Kolb *et al.* (2012b)] focus on solving the imbalance problem. But they rely on a data analysis phase before the matching job. It can perfectly solve the load balancing problem on MapReduce by adding an expensive cost before the matching process. Therefore, both these strategies are suitable for processing skewed data, but far more slow to deal with regular data or data with enormous size.

Review Selection. The efforts against information overload can be categorized into two groups. The first group selects complete reviews with high quality, and the second group deals with summarization on sentence or snippet level. For the first group, there are further two types of work, i.e., review ranking and selection, respectively. Review ranking ranks reviews according to their estimated quality, and chooses the top-*k* reviews as the result. Some of the methods are introduced as the review content-based work mentioned in credibility learning. So we just name a few here to raise the problems that cause the proposal of selection-based methods. Kim *et al.* (2006) train an SVM regression system on a variety of features to learn a helpfulness function, and apply it to automatically rank reviews. They also analyze the importance of different feature classes to capture review helpfulness, and find that the most useful features are the length, unigrams and product rating of a review. Hong *et al.* (2012) use user preference features to train a binary classifier and a SVM ranking system. The classifier divides reviews into helpful and helpless reviews, and the ranking system ranks reviews based on their helpfulness. Their evaluation shows that the user preference features improve the classification and ranking of reviews, and jointly using textual features proposed by Kim *et al.* (2006) can achieve further improvement. However, these methods suffer from low coverage of attributes as the resulting top-*k* reviews may contain redundant information. It is in that they estimate the review quality separately and do not consider the overall quality of the top-*k* reviews.

Review selection methods are thus proposed to select a set of reviews from the review collection of an item based on certain criteria. Lappas and Gunopulos (2010) propose to select a set of reviews that represent the majority opinions on attributes. The drawback of this approach is that it reduces the diversity of opinions, regardless of the fact that users tend to make purchase decision after viewing different opinions on an item. Tsaparas *et al.* (2011) intend to select a set of reviews that contain at least one positive and one negative opinion on each attribute. This method fails to reflect the distribution of opinions in the original review collection, thus misleading users. Lappas *et al.* (2012) proposed the selection of a set of reviews that capture the proportion of opinions in the entire review collection. The shortcoming of this approach falls in the lack of consideration on the quality of reviews. Furthermore, the three methods view all the attributes as the same, which may lead to the overload of attributes.

Review Summarization. The following group of work focuses on review summarization that generates opinion phrases for product features. Ganesan *et al.* (2012) propose to provide customers concise phrases instead of structured aspect-oriented pairs. Hu and Liu (2004) perform their work in three steps: first, mining review features; second, identifying opinion sentences; last, generating feature-based summaries. Zhuang *et al.* (2006) concentrate their summarization on movie reviews, and propose a multi-knowledge-based approach by using WordNet, statistical analysis and movie information. Meng and Wang (2009) extract product specifications from web sources, cluster these features and generate a feature tree for products. In such a case, it solves the problem of heterogeneity among schema and then maps each product to the same feature tree. The summarization is a tree with value attached along the leaves for each product. Moghaddam and Ester (2010) also suggest to generate an attribute table and provide summarized evaluations to these attributes. And then it can simplify users' reading and understanding to the products. Shimada *et al.* (2011) design a method for multi-aspects review summarization based on evaluative sentence extraction. It extracts the important aspects first, and then weights the surrounding sentences according to the TF–IDF values of the words within. Finally, it clusters these aspects by the topic similarity. Zhan *et al.* (2009) take almost the same steps as proposed by Shimada *et al.*

(2011) by identifying features from reviews, and grouping features into aspects. They all apply some rules to restrict the high frequency nouns in order to find the explicit features. However, Zhan *et al.* (2009) also take account of the low frequency words.

Unlike the above methods that identify nouns in reviews as features, some recent works discover latent aspects for review summarization. Latent aspect rating analysis (LARA) method is proposed by Wang *et al.* (2010) to estimate aspect weights from single user reviews. It assumes that a review's overall rating is a linear combination of the ratings on each aspect mentioned in the review. And it is extended by Wang *et al.* (2011) where latent aspects are estimated automatically. Topic model is combined with a hidden Markov model (HMM) as proposed by Sauper and Barzilay (2013) and Christina *et al.* (2011). Latent aspects and the corresponding sentiment ratings are discovered based on both the syntactic structures and semantic dependencies.

Though the aspect detection and opinion estimation in these works are related to ours, they are different from our work in processing granularity. So far, little attention is given to differentiating this summarization or opinion polarity by individual products or services. The work most similar to ours is explained by Sauper and Barzilay (2013). Although their model resembles ours on the snippet level, there are two key differences. First, the dishes of a restaurant are treated as aspects in their model, while dishes in our model comprise a high abstract level on top of different attributes, e.g., taste. Thus, their model only supports restaurant summarization. Second, their model utilizes bootstrap features to map words into scores, e.g., *good* → 5, which are used in the initialization step of their inference algorithm. Such bootstrap features depend on the language domain, and are generally difficult to extend to new languages.

Recommendation. Recommendation algorithm can be grouped into two types [Rajaraman and Ullman (2012)]: content-based recommendations and collaborative filtering (CF). The content-based approach builds a profile for each user or item to capture its properties [Blanco-Fernández *et al.* (2008)]. Then the profiles are used to predict whether a user likes an item. Compared with the content-based approach, the traditional collaborative filtering approach makes prediction based on the ratings expressed by similar users. Existing collaborative-filtering techniques [Sarwar *et al.* (2001); Koren *et al.* (2009); Koren and Bell (2011)] typically rely on analyzing users' past rating behavior to make predictions on new items for a user, in which the review text is not utilized. Particularly, probabilistic matrix factorization (PMF) methods [Salakhutdinov and Mnih (2007, 2008)] have been proved effective in real datasets [Bell and Koren (2007); Koren (2010); Koren *et al.* (2009); Ma *et al.* (2008); Wang and Blei (2011)]. While users care about the performance of recommendation, the improvement based on traditional CF method is limited and PMF fails at cold-start problem.

On the other hand, there has been ample work [Popescu and Etzioni (2005); Pang and Lee (2008); Titov and McDonald (2008a, 2008b); Brody and Elhadad (2010); Jo andOh (2011)] on review analysis from aspect discovery [Brody and Elhadad (2010); Jo and Oh (2011); Titov and McDonald (2008b)], sentiment analysis [Titov and McDonald (2008a)] to opinion mining [Popescu and Etzioni (2005); Pang and Lee (2008)], etc. However, none of them study the linkage between ratings and text reviews for making recommendations. Qu *et al.* (2010) and Ganu *et al.* (2009) study review rating prediction by combining text analysis techniques. Qu *et al.* (2010) model studies reviews using bag-of-opinions[6] representation, which is more expressive than unigram and N-gram representations. A linear model is then learned based on opinion roots, modifiers and negation words for review rating prediction. Ganu *et al.* (2009) model studies ratings as a function of pre-defined aspects and their polarities discovered from reviews. However, these two models are designed for predicting the rating of a given review, where user–item relationship is not captured. Therefore, they cannot be directly applied to a recommender system. Besides, the opinions learned by Qu *et al.* (2010) tend to be conclusive comments that convey little information about different aspects of a particular item.

Recent researches [Mei *et al.* (2007); Zhao *et al.* (2010); Wang *et al.* (2011)] incorporate LDA with hidden topics and sentiments to analyze reviews. These works provide a more fine-grained analysis of review text by separating sentiment words from neutral aspect words. Specially, Diao *et al.* (2014) build a language model component in his integrated

---

[6]An opinion here contains a subjectivity clue with positive or negative polarity.

model (JMARS) to uncover aspect-specific sentiment words in reviews. Therefore, JMARS is a probabilistic model based on collaborative filtering and topic modeling which is similar to ours. The work most related to ours is given by McAuley and Leskovec (2013), in which HFT is proposed to combine ratings with review text for product recommendation. HFT aligns hidden factors in ratings with hidden topics in reviews to create user/item profiles, which are then fit into SVD [Koren and Bell (2011)], a matrix factorization model to make rating predictions. The problem with HFT is that each time the review text is associated with one of the two dimensions, i.e., either from items' perspective (by grouping reviews by items) or from users' perspective (by grouping reviews by users), which means the hidden topics discovered only reflect the hidden factors of ratings from one dimension. The profiles of the other dimension are forced to be aligned to the same hidden factor space. We overcome this issue by proposing a novel model that considers both dimensions in discovering the common hidden factor space from review text.

1.4 Outline of Book Content

In this section, let us take a broad look at the outline of this book. In Chapter 2, we present an iterative algorithm to evaluate customer credibility on the scoring and review actions. It can be used to adjust the overall evaluation to products and find the useless reviews. In Chapter 3, we introduce two different kinds of methods for entity resolution, which will help a lot for entity management by finding the same products. One method is designed for centralized processing and the other one is for distributed processing. In Chapter 4, we suppose to select a small set of representative reviews for users by considering both the representativeness and diversity. In Chapter 5, instead of selecting a set of reviews, we summarize all the reviews of a product and generate summaries for each product. One method is to generate a concise snippet set and the relationship among those snippets is evaluated on a semantic hierarchical tree; the other method summarizes these snippets on different topics. In Chapter 6, we profile users and products based on the latent topics hidden inside reviews. We learn a model on topics to predict ratings and realize recommendation. Finally, we conclude the whole book in Chapter 7 and list the future work in review analysis.

Chapter 2

Credibility Learning

The open and dynamic E-commerce platforms start a convenient way for customers expressing the real opinion about the consumed products, which are represented as reviews and ratings. With the explosion of user-generated content (UGC), reviews and ratings have become an important element affecting financial benefit for online business. Then for competition, it may rise the generation of unfair or deceitful reviews and ratings. These reviews may affect the normal deals. Additionally, different customers, though believable, may have different credibilities to different kinds of products, e.g., professional or unprofessional. All consumers want to read the reviews from the professional customers. So, detecting trustful reviewers or generating authentic ratings for customers is urgent. In this chapter, we focus on the problem of customer credibility detection. We present a twin-bipartite graph model to catch the review and ranking relationship among users, products and shops; we design a feedback mechanism to get consistent ranking among users and products; customer credibility are adjusted by feedback considering rating consistency, and ratings are recalculated through combining customer credibility together with originally assigned ratings.

2.1 Problem Definition

In this section, we give a detailed definition to customer credibility. Then we present the background knowledge to demonstrate its usefulness.

2.1.1 *Problem Description*

User-generated reviews play an important role in decision-making process for those who are trying to buy products online, as online commercial activities continue to grow [Mulpuru (2008)]. However, there is an increasing number of reviews available, making it difficult to check all the reviews for online shopping. Before reading all the reviews of items in detail, it is common to rank the candidates and decide which one to check. The ranking is usually based on the overall scores by averaging individual review scores given by previous customers [Medo and Wakeling (2010); Li *et al.* (2012)]. Then customers may click on items that attract them. However, when calculating the average scores for items, it takes each review score as evenly trustworthy. In real-world systems, there exist many unfair/improper ratings for the big financial benefits coming from reviews and ratings, which may be caused by either subjectivity or maliciousness [Zhang *et al.* (2008); Sabater and Sierra (2005); Dellarocas (2000)], including "ballot stuffing", "bad-mouthing" [Dellarocas (2000)], and so on.

Some customers do not give out fair evaluations to the products which they have purchased. They may be prone to give gentle evaluations [Tsur and Rappoport (2009)]. Some customers may not be serious to reviews by assigning random score to products, and some customers may always give the maximal/minimal scores. At worst, some of them assigns totally bad evaluations to products from competitors and completely good evaluations to products from collaborators, which is known as spammers [Li *et al.* (2014b); Mukherjee *et al.* (2013b)]. Though credibility-based scoring has been designed [Medo and Wakeling (2010); Li *et al.* (2012)], it computes customer credibility as defined in Definition 2.1 based on the inconsistency between the individual scores and the single overall score. But it does not consider the relationship between customer credibility and quality of products. Additionally, inconsistency also occurs between review comment and review score. It means that a review with a high score has a negative review comment. A full-fledged credibility calculation algorithm is still missing.

Definition 2.1 (Customer Credibility (*Cred*(*c*) for customer *c*)). It is defined as the confidence to believe the customer *c*'s reviews including both review comments and scores with $0 \leq Cred(c) \leq 1$. $Cred(c) = 0$ and 1 represent spammers and professionals, respectively.

In this chapter, we propose to design a new framework for evaluating customer credibility. We try to resolve the review inconsistency problem between review content and review score. By analyzing the review data, we try to catch individual credibility (honesty). It is totally complementary to previous incentive-design work [Miller *et al.* (2005); Jurca and Faltings (2003); Papaioannou and Stamoulis (2005); Jurca and Faltings (2004)]. We give a comprehensive description to our method, and add new experiment results together with in-depth analysis. We propose an Maximum Entropy-based (ME-based) method to correct the inconsistency between review score and comment. Newly autopredicted scores may be used as the customer review scores for calculating the overall scores. We explore the shopping and reviewing behaviors to evaluate the customer credibility. Over a twin-bipartite shopping-reviewing graph, we propose to evaluate customers honesty using credibility. We measure user credibility using the aggregated difference between individual rating and the overall product ratings. A feedback mechanism is defined to catch the difference when updating credibilities. We propose to combine the scores from semantic level and numerical level analysis. The basic idea behind is: good products deserve to receive high review scores while bad ones should be given low scores; good customers, should give high scores to good products and low scores to bad ones.

2.1.2 *Background*

Review Graph. We have three types of vertices: shops, products and customers, as shown in Fig. 2.1. The edges in the graph represent the transaction relationships with reviews (comment and score) attached along each edge. Formally, let $G_{PCS} = \{P, C, S, E_{PC}, E_{SC}\}$ be a graph, where P, S and C denotes the set of products, shops and customers, respectively, E_{PC} denotes the links between P and C, and E_{SC} denotes the links between S and C. The attachment r between products/shops and customers is a piece of review including comment x and score w. Edge $e_{c \to p} \in E_{PC}$ has weight $w_{c \to p}$. We say that customer c gives the review r with score $w_{c \to p}$ to

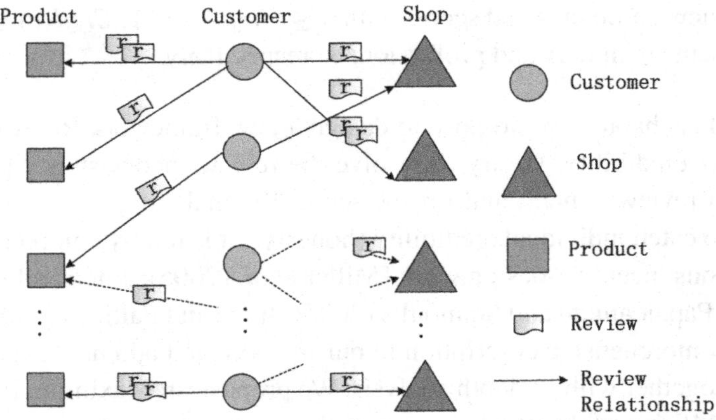

Fig. 2.1: Product–Customer–Shop (PCS) Graph

Table 2.1: Table of Notations

Expression	Description
$w_{c\to p}$ OR $w_{c\to p}^{CA}$	customer c gives the review r with score $w_{c\to p}$ to product p
$w_{c\to p}^{ME}$	predicted score from customer c to product p by ME method
$w_{c\to s}$	customer c gives the review r with score $w_{c\to s}$ to shop s
C_p	set of customers giving reviews to product p
C_s	set of customers giving reviews to shop s
P_c	set of products receiving reviews from customer c
S_c	set of shops receiving reviews from customer c
R_p	set of reviews for product p
R_s	set of reviews for shop s
$\|\bullet\|$	the number of set $\bullet$
$Cred(c)$	credibility of customer c
$Score(p)$	overall score of product p
$Score(s)$	overall score of shop s
P_G, P_B, P_N	good product set, bad product set and others (normal ones)
S_G, S_B, S_N	good shop set, bad shop set and others (normal ones)

product p. Edge $e_{c\to s} \in E_{SC}$ has weight $w_{c\to s}$. We say that customer c gives the review r with score $w_{c\to s}$ to shop s. In order to make it easy to introduce the following sections, we display the notations used in the following parts in Table 2.1.

In our calculation, we normalize review scores and keep them in the range of $[-1, 1]$. Also, we normalize customer credibility values and keep them in the range of $[0, 1]$.

Credibility-based Scoring. Generally, the overall evaluations of products and shops are calculated by summarizing the review scores from customers. For product p, its overall rating score is calculated as:

$$Score^o(p) = \begin{cases} \dfrac{\sum_{c \in C_p}(w_{c \to p})}{|C_p|}, & |C_p| > 0 \\ defaultV, & |C_p| = 0. \end{cases}$$

Similarly, for shop s, the original overall score is:

$$Score^o(s) = \begin{cases} \dfrac{\sum_{c \in C_s}(w_{c \to s})}{|C_s|}, & |C_s| > 0 \\ defaultV, & |C_s| = 0, \end{cases}$$

where $defaultV$ is generally set to max (5 star) in the review system.

As we mentioned above, some customers do not score fairly. Thus, such kinds of evaluations may lead to wrong results. So, we propose to consider customer credibilities as the weights when computing the overall scores. For product p and shop s, their overall scores weighted with customer credibilities are modified as:

$$Score(p) = \begin{cases} \dfrac{\sum_{c \in C_p}(Cred(c) \times w_{c \to p})}{|C_p|}, & |C_p| > 0 \\ defaultV, & |C_p| = 0 \end{cases}$$

and

$$Score(s) = \begin{cases} \dfrac{\sum_{c \in C_s}(Cred(c) \times w_{c \to s})}{|C_s|}, & |C_s| > 0 \\ defaultV, & |C_s| = 0, \end{cases}$$

where $Cred(c)$ is the credibility value of customer c, calculated in Section 2.4.

Customer credibility is used to alleviate the influence of noisy reviews. It is normalized in the range of [0, 1] following,

$$c' = \begin{cases} \dfrac{c - c_{min}}{c_{max} - c_{min}}, & c_{max} \neq c_{min} \\ cred_{def}, & c_{max} = c_{min}, \end{cases} \tag{2.1}$$

where $cred_{def}$ is the default credibility value with value 0.5.

For product score, we normalize it in the range of $[-1, 1]$ following,

$$Score' = \frac{Score(i) - 3}{2}, \tag{2.2}$$

supposing we score the item $Score(i)$ by five levels from 1 to 5.

2.2 Scoring Framework Overview

Figure 2.2 shows the framework of our approach, which contains three modules corresponding to the following three tasks:

(1) **Review Comment Analysis:** To predict the rating scores from review comments.

(2) **Customer Credibility Analysis:** To analyze the credibility of customers by exploring shopping and reviewing behaviors on the PCS graph.

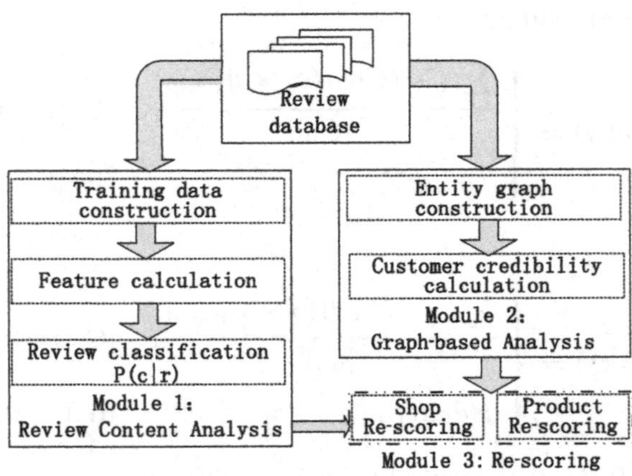

Fig. 2.2: Framework of Re-scoring Approach

(3) **Re-scoring:** To re-score the products and shops by combining the predicted scores from review comments and customer credibility.

Review Comment Analysis (Module 1): The main purpose is to check inconsistency between the original review scores (numerical level) and the comments (semantic level) and predict the new scores based on the comments themselves. This step of work ensures the correctness, usefulness and validity of the work in Modules 2 and 3. In this part of work, we use supervised learning technologies to predict the scores. The details are described in Section 2.3.

Customer Credibility Analysis (Module 2): The main purpose is to analyze the credibility of customers. We use the PCS graph to model the relationship among products, shops and customers. Then we design iteration algorithms to calculate the scores of products/shops and the credibility of customers interactively. This module is the main part of our approach and the details are described in Section 2.4.

Re-scoring (Module 3): The main purpose is to re-score both the products and shops based on the predicted scores from Module 1 and the customer credibility from Module 2. The details are described in Section 2.5.

2.3 Review Comment Analysis

We use a classifier to predict the score of the review comment. The classifier is built based on Maximum Entropy (ME) model [Berger *et al.* (1996); Nigam *et al.* (1999)]. Note that we can also apply other supervised learning models, such as Support Vector Machines (SVM) [Vapnik (1995)] and Naïve Bayes [Mitchell (1997)] in our approach. In this work, we call these scores of review comments as ME-predicted scores, $w^{ME}_{c\to p}$ and the original review scores as customer-assigned scores, $w^{CA}_{c\to p}$.

We first introduce the ME model and define the templates for feature representation. To train the model, we need labeled training data that are troublesome to obtain, because of the high cost of human annotation. Then, we design a way to construct the training data automatically instead of human annotation. Finally, we train a ME classifier on the training data and predict the scores for all the comments.

2.3.1 *ME Model*

ME model has been successfully applied to various classification tasks including text categorization and Part-of-Speech tagging with the state-of-the-art accuracies [Berger *et al.* (1996); Nigam *et al.* (1999)]. The basic idea behind ME is that one should prefer the uniform models that also satisfy any given constraints. In its most general formulation, the ME model can be used to estimate any probability distribution. Here, we are interested in scoring the input examples by the binary classification way. That is, we learn conditional distributions from labeled training data. Specifically, we learn the probability distribution of the classes (positive and negative) given a review content.

With the constraints (features) given the training data, there is a unique distribution that has ME. In general, a conditional ME model is an log-linear model as follows:

$$p(y|x) = \frac{1}{Z(x)} \exp\left(\sum_i (\lambda_i f_i(x, y))\right), \tag{2.3}$$

where each $f_i(x, y)$ is a feature, y is the class, λ_i is a parameter to be estimated and $Z(x)$ is simply the normalizing factor to ensure proper probability:

$$Z(x) = \sum_t \exp\left(\sum_i (\lambda_i f_i(x, y))\right). \tag{2.4}$$

Then, we define feature templates to generate the features for Equation (2.3). Table 2.2 lists the feature templates we use in our experiments. There are three types of features: (1) Base Feature that considers the basic information of comments; (2) Part-of-Speech Feature that considers the Part-of-Speech tags of words; (3) Emotion Feature that considers the information of emotion words.[1] We use an example to demonstrate how to generate the features. For the template "FirstRev" of

[1]In the experiments, we use an emotion word dictionary that is available at http://www.keenage.com/html/c_index.html.

Table 2.2: Feature Templates

Feature	Description
	Review-based Features
FirstRev	It is the first review
OnlyRev	It is the only review
TokenNum	Number of tokens
SentNum	Number of sentences
UniqWordRat	Ratio of unique words
AveSentLen	Average sentence length
RevDate	The days between the shop opening and this reviews
DeviatCusRev	Deviation from customer average rating
Unigram	Each word
bigram	Bigram word combination
	Review Part-of-Speech Feature
NN	Ratio of nouns
ADJ	Ratio of adjectives
COMP	Ratio of comparatives
V	Ratio of verbs
RB	Ratio of adverbs
SYM	Ratio of symbols
CD	Ratio of numbers
PP	Ratio of punctuations
	Review Emotion Feature
UniEmotion	Each emotion word
EmotionType	Emotion type of each emotion word
PosWordRat	Ratio of positive words
NegWordRat	Ratio of negative words

Base Feature, we have a binary feature function:

$$f(x, y) = \begin{cases} 1, & \text{if (it is the first review)} \\ 0, & \text{otherwise.} \end{cases}$$

We select the combination of feature templates for the final systems by tuning on the development dataset.

2.3.2 *Constructing Labeled Data*

To train an ME model, we need a set of labeled examples as the training data. However, labeling the data is hard because of the high cost of human annotation. We design a method to construct the training data that include negative and positive examples.

For negative examples, we choose the reviews with low review scores. We investigate the data collected from some customer-to-customer (C2C) sites and find that for reviews with low scores, the customers always write negative words to express opinions in the comments. There are few cases in which customers write good comments with low scores. And this is consistent with the review mechanism in these C2C platforms, e.g., Taobao or Gmarket. In these review systems, reviewing is not allowed unless you bought something. Though paying for lowering competitors' ratings is possible by assigning bad reviews called *negative fake*, it is not practical, especially among a large set of reviews.

But for positive examples, the above method does not work because of the following two reasons:

- *positive fake1*: Buying for good reviews is possible and practical, e.g., from friends and families;
- *positive fake2*: Mismatching of scores and comments is generally existing as discussed before.

One important observation is that in the same shop, the repeat customers are always positive to the bought products. Here, "repeat" means buying the same products or some other products in the same shop more than once. The intuition behind this is that satisfied customer will come back. In order to reduce the influence of *positive fake1*, the member c in selected repeat customers C shall satisfy the following rules:

Rule 1 (Representativeness). $S_c \geq ShopN$, $ShopN > 0$. c has visited at least *ShopN* different shops and is experienced. Default *ShopN* is set to 5. c is supposed to experience more than one shop.

Rule 2 (Diversity). $\exists p, p \in P_c$ *and* $R_p \geq ReviewN$, $ReviewN > 0$. $ReviewN$ is the number of reviews from distinct customers. Default $ReviewN$ is set to 10. c is supposed to visit popular shops/products.

Rule 3 (Consistency). $\ell = max\left(\frac{DifL_p^c}{DifG_p^c}, DifL_p^c, DifG_p^c\right)$. ℓ denotes the consistency of reviewers. $DifL_p^c$ and $DifG_p^c$ are defined in Equation (2.5). c is supposed to have the same rating ability with others. $DifL_p^c$ and $DifG^c$

represent the local and global difference degrees with other reviewers. For C, we rank these members by their ℓ values in descending order and filter the top W ones. Default W is set to 10.

$$DifL_p^c = \left| \frac{W_{c \to p}}{Score(p)} - 1 \right|; \quad DifG_p^c = \frac{\sum_{|P_c|} DifL_p}{|P_c|}. \tag{2.5}$$

We use **Rules 1–3** to select the good reviewers that are experienced (Rule 1), active (Rule 2) and trustful (Rule 3).

2.3.3 *Training and Prediction*

We use the feature templates in Table 2.2 to perform feature representation for the above data. We then use MaxEnt,[2] a freely available implementation of ME, to train our classifier. Given a review comment, the classifier can predict a score in [0, 1] for each class (positive and negative). The predicted class y^* is:

$$y^* = argmax_y(p(y|x)). \tag{2.6}$$

Thus, the final ME-predicted score for review x given by customer c to product p is:

$$w_{c \to p}^{ME} = \begin{cases} p(y^*|x), & y^* \text{ is positive} \\ -p(y^*|x), & y^* \text{ is negative.} \end{cases}$$

2.4 Customer Credibility Calculation

Customer credibility is used to catch to what extent we can believe the review given by the customer. A twin-bipartite graph is used to model the review relationship among customer, shop and product. The following ideas are well supported in our design:

(1) Customers writing good (bad) reviews to good (bad) products are the credible customers and customers writing good (bad) reviews to bad (good) products are incredible;

[2] http://homepages.inf.ed.ac.uk/lzhang10/maxent_toolkit.html.

(2) Good products should receive high review scores from the credible customers while bad products should receive low scores from the credible customers. Shops meet the similar situation.

Based on the PCS graph of Fig. 2.1, we design the algorithms to calculate the credibility for all the customers. In our algorithms:

(1) If good (bad) products/shops are given low (high) scores by a customer, we give a negative feedback to reduce the credibility of the customer.
(2) If good (bad) products/shops are given high (low) scores by a customer, we give a positive feedback to improve the credibility of the customer.

We first use the relationship between the products and customers for calculating the customer credibility. Then, we use the relationship between the shops and customers. Finally, we combine them to seek the balance.

2.4.1 *Product and Customer*

Here, we will introduce the algorithm to calculate the credibility for all the customers based on the relationship between the products and the customers. The score of a product depends on the scores given by its customers and the credibilities of these customers while the credibility in turn depends on the feedback from products. Thus, to solve this, we take the method of fixed-point iteration on the graph. We denote the credibility of customer c and the score of product p at iteration n^{th} by $Cred_P^n(c)$ and $Score^n(p)$ respectively. We compute the values for iteration $(n+1)^{\text{th}}$ using the values obtained at iteration n^{th}. One iteration has two phases: product-scoring and credibility-calculating. We initialize the credibility values randomly and get credibility initial vector Υ. The iteration is finished when the change of the credibility is small than predefined threshold $\delta, 0 \leq \delta < 1$.

- **Product-scoring:** For each product p, its score $Score(p)$ is the overall score by considering its customer scores and the customer credibilities. So for p, its $(n+1)^{\text{th}}$ score is:

$$Score^{n+1}(p) = \frac{\sum_{c \in C_p} \left(Cred_P^n(c) \times w_{c \to p}\right)}{|C_p|}. \tag{2.7}$$

- **Credibility-calculating:** We perform feedback only on the good and bad products which are the most highly scored and the most lowly scored respectively. First, we order the products decreasingly by current scores. Then, we select the top $t\%$ and bottom $t\%$ products as the representative products for good and bad ones into P_G and P_B, respectively, where t is a threshold that will be tuned on the development data. The rest of products are classified as normal and put into set P_N. We use X_p to evaluate the consistency to good and bad classifications. X_p is in the range of [0, 1] that defined as follows:

$$X_p^{n+1} = \begin{cases} \dfrac{Score^{n+1}(p) - min_{PG}}{max_{PG} - min_{PG}} & \text{if } (p \in P_G \text{ and } max_{PG} \neq min_{PG}) \\ \dfrac{max_{PB} - Score^{n+1}(p)}{max_{PB} - min_{PB}} & \text{if } (p \in P_B \text{ and } max_{PB} \neq min_{PB}) \\ 0.5 & \text{if } (max_{PG} = min_{PG} \\ & \quad \text{or } max_{PB} = min_{PB}) \\ 0 & \text{others,} \end{cases}$$

where max_{PG} and min_{PG} are the maximum and minimum scores in P_G respectively, while max_{PB} and min_{PB} are the maximum and minimum scores in P_B respectively. The feedback value from p to c is:

$$Fb_{p\to c}^{n+1} = \begin{cases} (w_{c\to p} - w_N) \times X_p^{n+1} & \text{if } (p \in P_G) \\ -(w_{c\to p} - w_N) \times X_p^{n+1} & \text{if } (p \in P_B) \\ 0 & \text{if } (p \in P_N), \end{cases}$$

where w_N is the average score for normal products. Thus, the feedback value is measured by X_p and the difference between the customer score and the normal score. From the above equation, we can see that when a product is normal, its feedback value becomes zero and it does not affect customer credibility. Otherwise, it gives a positive or negative feedback value to its customer credibilities. For a good product, its customer receives a positive (negative) feedback value if the customer gives a positive (negative) score. Similarly, for a bad product, its customer receives a positive (negative) feedback value if the customer gives a negative (positive) score. Then, the credibility of customer c at iteration $(n+1)^{\text{th}}$ is calculated by combining the feedback values as:

$$Cred_P^{n+1}(c) = \frac{\sum_{p \in P_c} \left(Fb_{p \to c}^{n+1} \right)}{|P_c|}. \tag{2.8}$$

2.4.2 *Shop and Customer*

We also use the relationship between shops and customers to calculate the credibility of the customers in the similar manner. We denote the credibility of customer c and the score of shop p at iteration n by $Cred_S^n(c)$ and $Score^n(s)$ respectively. We also have two phases in one iteration: shop-scoring and credibility-calculating.

- **Shop-scoring:** The score of shop s is:

$$Score^{n+1}(s) = \frac{\sum_{c \in C_s} Cred_S^n(c) \times w_{c \to s}}{|C_s|}. \tag{2.9}$$

- **Credibility-calculating:** We perform feedback only on the good and bad shops which are the most highly scored and the most lowly scored respectively. First, we order the shops decreasingly to a list. Then, we select the top $t\%$ and bottom $t\%$ shops as the representative shops for good and bad ones into S_G and S_B, respectively, where t is a threshold. The rest of the products are classified as normal and put into set S_N. We also define X_s to calculate the feedback values:

$$X_s^{n+1} = \begin{cases} \dfrac{Score^{n+1}(s) - min_{SG}}{max_{SG} - min_{SG}} & \text{if } (s \in S_G \text{ and } max_{SG} \neq min_{SG}) \\ \dfrac{max_{SB} - Score^{n+1}(s)}{max_{SB} - min_{SB}} & \text{if } (s \in S_B \text{ and } max_{SB} \neq min_{SB}) \\ 0.5 & \text{if } (max_{SG} = min_{SG} \\ & \quad \text{or } max_{SB} = min_{SB}) \\ 0 & \text{if } (s \in S_N), \end{cases}$$

where max_{SG} and min_{SG} are the maximum and minimum scores in S_G respectively while max_{SB} and min_{SB} are the maximum and minimum scores in S_B respectively.

The feedback value from s to c is:

$$Fb_{s\to c}^{n+1} = \begin{cases} (w_{c\to s} - w_N) \times X_s^{n+1} & \text{if } (s \in S_G) \\ -(w_{c\to s} - w_N) \times X_s^{n+1} & \text{if } (s \in S_B) \\ 0 & \text{if } (s \in S_N). \end{cases}$$

Then, the credibility of customer c at iteration $(n+1)$th is calculated by considering the feedback values.

$$Cred_S^{n+1}(c) = \frac{\sum_{s\in S_c}(Feedbk^{n+1}(s \to c))}{|S_c|}, \tag{2.10}$$

where S_c is the set of shops in which c buys products.

2.4.3 *Credibility Calculation*

In the above sections, we calculate the credibilities on each SingleGraphs (graph G_{PC} and G_{SC}). Here, we take the linear model to combine these two results, since it is easy to fit the parameters. We can take the combined result in each round of calculation (on the twinGraph). At iteration n^{th}, the combined credibility is:

$$Cred_B^n(c) = \alpha \cdot Cred_P^n(c) + (1-\alpha) \cdot Cred_S^n(c), \quad 0 \le \alpha \le 1. \tag{2.11}$$

2.5 Re-scoring

Finally, we obtain the credibility value $Cred(c)$ for each customer c and have two types of review scores: (1) Semantic Level $w_{c\to p}^{ME}$, ME-predicted score; (2) Numerical Level $w_{c\to p}^{CA}$, customer-assigned score.

We calculate the new overall score of product p by the following equation:

$$Score^{ME}(p) = \frac{\sum_{c\in C_p}\left(Cred(c) \times w_{c\to p}^{ME}\right)}{|C_p|} \tag{2.12}$$

or

$$Score^{CA}(p) = \frac{\sum_{c\in C_p}\left(Cred(c) \times w_{c\to p}^{CA}\right)}{|C_p|}. \tag{2.13}$$

Similarly, for shop s, the overall score is:

$$Score^{ME}(s) = \frac{\sum_{c \in C_s} \left(Cred(c) \times w_{c \to s}^{ME}\right)}{|C_s|} \quad (2.14)$$

or

$$Score^{CA}(s) = \frac{\sum_{c \in C_s} \left(Cred(c) \times w_{c \to s}^{CA}\right)}{|C_s|}. \quad (2.15)$$

2.6 Experimental Results

In this section, we describe in detail the experiments conducted on real datasets using our proposed approach. The main purpose is to evaluate our ranking system and compare it with the previous studies. We also evaluate the accuracy of review comment analysis on the data.

2.6.1 *Datasets*

We collect the data from the Taobao site that is the biggest Chinese C2C E-commerce site. In Taobao, only the customers who have purchased a product can write a comment and assign a score (customer-assigned score) to the product.

The collected data include 15 categories, such as “clothes and shoes”, “books”, and so on. There are 553,000 customers, 300,000 products, 10,000 shops and 924,000 reviews after we preprocess the data. Each review contains the comment, the evaluation score, the customer who writes it, the product and the shop.

We check the transaction distributions. Customer transaction distributions are consistent to the long-tail distribution as shown in Fig. 2.3. Most of the customers have just a few online transactions. From the figure, we find that 70% of the customers transacted only once, while 11% transacted more than three times. We also check product transaction distribution as shown in Fig. 2.3(b). The figure shows most of the products have one or two transactions. These facts indicate that most of the customers do not have any preference shops and they have to depend on the product/shop ranking system to search for the candidates. We remove the products (shops) that have only one transaction from the data.

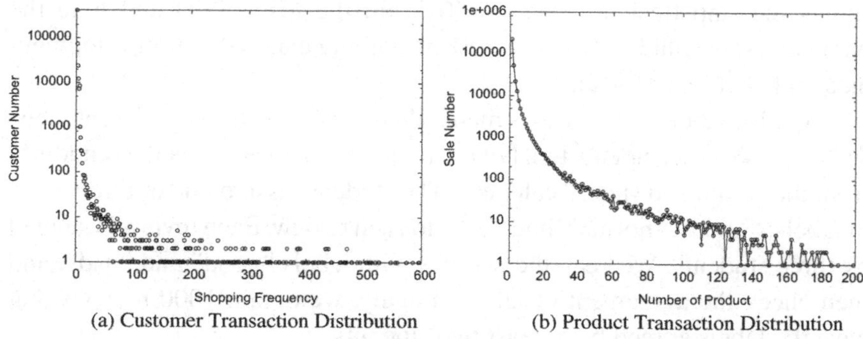

(a) Customer Transaction Distribution (b) Product Transaction Distribution

Fig. 2.3: Transaction Distributions

Table 2.3: Statistics of Data for ME Model

Type	Repeat Type	Num
Positive	SoftBuy	33113
	HardBuy	17766
Negative	N/A	5950

2.6.2 *Review Comment Analysis*

In this section, we evaluate the accuracy of comment prediction given by the ME-based models. First, we describe the data for evaluation. Second, we introduce the evaluation measure. Finally, we show the experimental results and illustrate some examples with predicted scores. In this section, for adjusting the weight between the credibilities calculated by G_{PC} graph and G_{SC} graph in Equation (2.11), we set $\alpha = 0.5$ and take them equally.

Data for Comment Analysis. As described in Section 2.3, we construct the labeled data automatically. The positive examples are based on the reviews given by the repeat customers with high customer-assigned scores and the negative examples are the ones with low scores. We define two repeat types: "SoftBuy" and "HardBuy" that are defined by the re-shopping interval with repeat interval "$\geq$1 day" and "$\geq$5 days", respectively. Table 2.3

shows the statistical information. To train the ME model and tune the parameters, we randomly select 70% as training data, 10% as development data and 20% as test data.

We also label some reviews manually to evaluate from a different view. We invite several students to label the reviews which are selected randomly from the "cloth and shoes" category. The students assign one of three types of labels: "good", "normal" and "bad" to each review. Each review is labeled by three students. We keep the reviews with labels "good" and "bad", and then check the agreement of labels. Finally, we obtain 1000 reviews that have the labels agreed by at least two students.

We call the manual data as *TestMan* data and the automatic generated test data as *TestAuto* data. Both datasets are used in the evaluation.

Evaluation Metrics. We evaluate the ME-based classifier by two ways: automatic and manual methods. The difference is which data we use for testing. For the automatic method, we use *TestAuto* data as the test data. For the manual method, we use *TestMan* data.

We measure the classifier quality by the accuracy:

$$accuracy = \frac{N_c}{N},$$

where N_c is the number of comments with correct labels and N is the number of comment in the test set.

Results of Automatic Method. We train the ME model with different types of features (as defined in Table 2.2) on the trained data and select the best feature combination on the development data. We first show the accuracies for all the categories in Figs. 2.4 and 2.5 and the average accuracies in Fig. 2.6 on the development data. From the figures, we find that the results of the SoftBuy (Fig. 2.5) is better than the HardBuy (Fig. 2.4). The reason is that the number of reviews in the SoftBuy is larger than the HardBuy, which can usually result in better performance in supervised learning. The models with Base features plus Emotion features perform the best, especially for the HardBuy that has less data. From Figs. 2.4 and 2.5, we can see that when we use both the Base Features and Part-of-Speech Features, it will decrease the performance in most of the cases. And in Fig. 2.6, the average accuracy

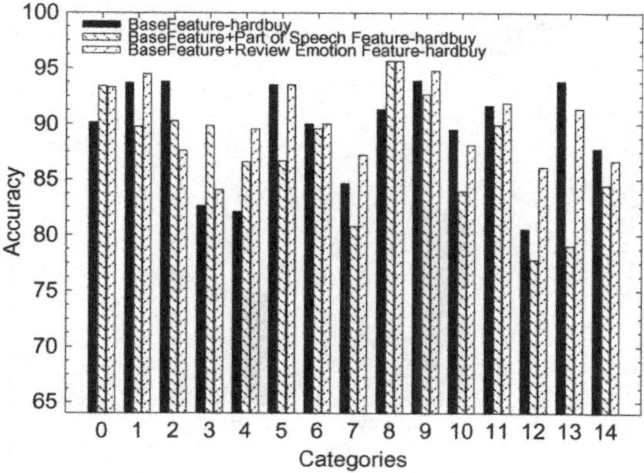

Fig. 2.4: Feature Combinations on Development Data (HardBuy)

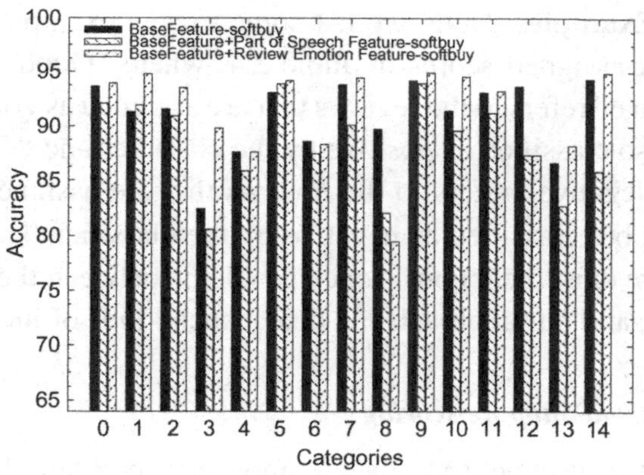

Fig. 2.5: Feature Combinations on Development Data (SoftBuy)

will also be decreased by using the Part-of-Speech Features. Thus, we use the Base Features and Emotion Features in our following experiments.

Then, we evaluate the classifier on the *TestAuto* data. The accuracy is 91.4% for the SoftBuy data and 90.2% for the HardBuy data.

Results of Manual Method. We also evaluate the classifier, which is trained on the HardBuy data and on the *TestMan* data. The accuracy is 85.2% which is little lower than the score (90%) of the automatic method for the same category.

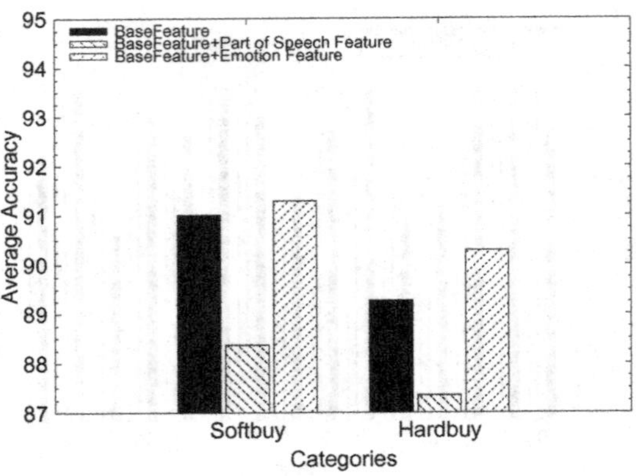

Fig. 2.6: Average Accuracy on Development Data

Illustration Examples. Here, we list some review examples which have high customer-assigned scores in Table 2.4, where "Good Reviews with Content Positive" refers to the reviews that are assigned as good by the customers and also classified as positive by the classifier and "Good Reviews but Content Negative" refers to the reviews that are assigned as good by the customers but classified as negative by the classifier. These examples show that there exist the inconsistency problems between the review score and comment, and our approach can detect such kinds of inconsistencies.

2.6.3 *Product and Shop Re-scoring*

How to get the ground truth is an important problem for evaluating the ranking algorithms [Li *et al.* (2012)]. In practice, no ground truth products/shops ranking is available in advance. In previous studies, they have to use a baseline system to generate a ranking list as the ground truth [Li *et al.* (2012)]. This method is hard to judge how good the new algorithms are.

In this work, we use real data to generate the ground truth. We rely on the following assumptions:

- The products having the repeat customers are good products with a higher probability than other products.
- The shops having the repeat customers are good shops with a higher probability than others.

Table 2.4: Illustration Examples of Good Reviews with Positive and Negative Review Content

S.No.	Review
	Good Reviews with Content Positive
1	The quality is good and valuable (质量还不错物有所值).
2	The shoes are light and comfortable (鞋子很轻,很舒服).
3	The quality is good and worthy. Then I suppose to check this shop whenever want to buy something for my husband (质量非常好,很值,打算下回给老公买东东先来他家看看).
4	The quality is fantastic. It is worthy to buy this kind of shoes in such a cost (质量超好,这个价格可以买到这种质量的鞋子,真给力).
5	It is very practical and the dealer is good (很实用,卖家服务态度很好很热情).
	Good Reviews but Content Negative
1	The craftsmanship of the shoes is average and the express is slow (鞋子做工很一般,快递太慢,勉强好评).
2	Some described functionalities are not found (有些描述上的功能没有找到).
3	Calling 10010, it says there is 5-yuan a month-rental and after February 2012, it will be 14-yuan a month-rental. It is different with what the dealer says (打10010询问,现在有5元月租,2012年2月后为14 元月租与卖家说的0月租不相符)).
4	Be careful and I am cheated to be this shop (各位千万要小心了。我是被骗来买的,希望大家多留个心眼).
5	The instruction is different with the watch and I still do not know how to use it (说明书和手表不配套,我还没学会).

Data for Product and Shop Re-scoring. We extract the products and the shops which have the repeat customers following the three rules introduced in Section 2.3, from the collected data. Table 2.5 shows the statistical information of products and shops, where “ProdNum” and “ShopNum” are the numbers of products and shops having the repeat customers, and “CustNum” and “UniqCustNum” are total numbers of customers and unique customers having the repeat customers (for the same product or in the same shop). To select the parameters for the systems, we randomly select 30% of the products/shops as development data and others as test data.

Evaluation Metrics. After obtaining the ground truth, we evaluate the systems as follows. We first calculate the scores of the products (shops). Then, we sort the products (shops) in decreasing order by the scores

Table 2.5: Repeat Customer Statistics

	Repeat Type	ProdNum	CustNum	UniqCustNum
Product	SoftBuy	1330	1975	957
	HardBuy	902	1233	803
	Repeat Type	ShopNum	CustNum	UniqCustNum
Shop	SoftBuy	3445	12071	6917
	HardBuy	1897	5994	3805

and calculate the number of products (shops) N_k having the repeat customers among the TOP $K\%$ in the sorted list. The evaluation metric is: $B_k@TOPK = N_k/N_{all}$, where N_{all} is the total number of products (shops) having the repeat customers.

According to assumption, the expectation is that the products (shops) with higher scores should have more chances to have the repeat customers. That is, if method M_a has the higher percentages of the products having repeat customers in high score areas (such as TOP 10%, 20%, 30%) than method M_b, we say M_a is better than M_b.

Baselines:

(1) **Arithmetic average algorithm (AA).** It ranks the products/shops by the average customer-assigned scores as defined by $Score^o p$ and $Score^o s$. AA is a popular method for ranking in IR community and easy to be implemented [Medo and Wakeling (2010); Li *et al.* (2012)].
(2) **HITS algorithm.** We use the HITS algorithm proposed by Deng *et al.* (2009) designed for bipartite graphs.
(3) **L1-AVG algorithm.** It also takes an iterative approach for bipartite rating networks proposed by Li *et al.* (2012).

Parameters Selection and Verification. We test the influence of parameters δ and t in the algorithms to system performance on the development data. The experiments are run on the twinGraph with the ME-predicted scores. Figures 2.7(a) and 2.7(b) show the results. When $\delta < 10^{-6}$ and $t < 30\%$, the accuracy changes obviously but it does not change so much

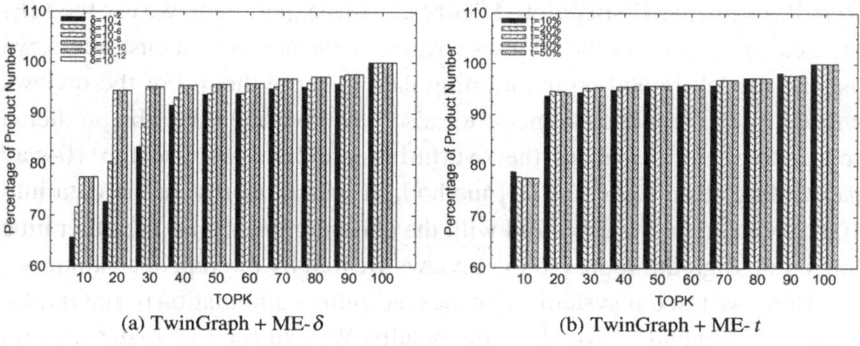

(a) TwinGraph + ME-δ

(b) TwinGraph + ME- t

Fig. 2.7: Parameter Tests

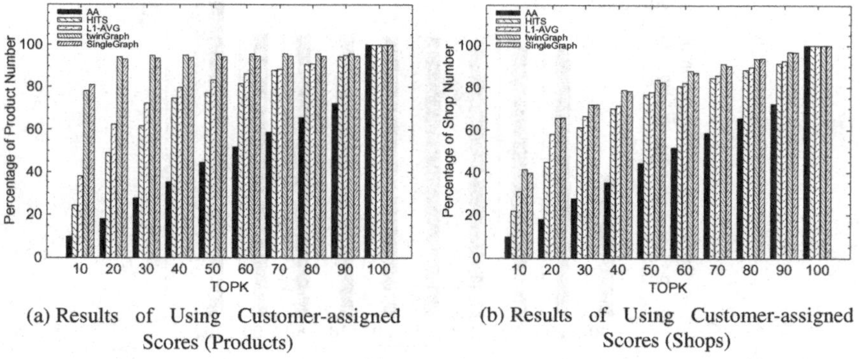

(a) Results of Using Customer-assigned Scores (Products)

(b) Results of Using Customer-assigned Scores (Shops)

Fig. 2.8: Results of using Customer-assigned Scores

when they exceed these values. In the following experiments, we use the settings: $\delta = 10^{-6}$ and $t = 30\%$.

Results of using Customer-assigned Scores. In this experiment, we use the customer-assigned scores. The results are shown in Figs. 2.8(a) and 2.8(b), where "twinGraph" refers to the method of using the credibility combination (G_{PCS} — twin bipartite graph) and "SingleGraph" refers to the method of using the individual credibility (G_{PC}/G_{SC} — single bipartite graph). For the products, we find that twinGraph performs the best and SingleGraph outperforms the baseline systems. And for the shops, twinGraph performs a little better than SingleGraph.

Results of using ME-predicted Scores. In this experiment, we use the ME-predicated scores. For the reviews written by the non-repeat customers, we use the model trained on the training data to score them. For the reviews written by the repeat customers, we also have to assign the ME-predicted scores to them. To avoid the overfitting problem, we use the 10-way jackknifing [Koo *et al.* (2008)] method, in which we divide the data into 10 folds and then tag each fold with the classifier trained on the other nine folds, to assign the scores to the reviews written by the repeat customers.

Here, we test our systems with the credibility combination (twinGraph). Figures 2.9(a) and 2.9(b) show the results. We can see that using reviews

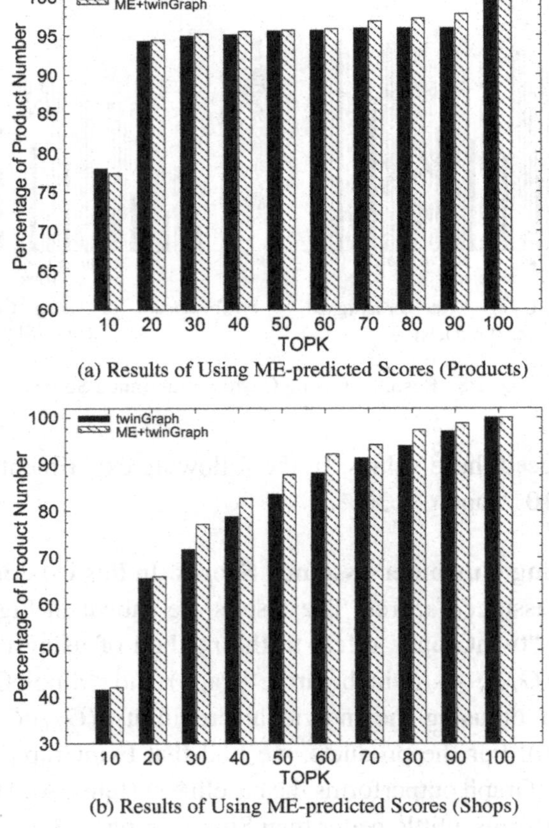

(a) Results of Using ME-predicted Scores (Products)

(b) Results of Using ME-predicted Scores (Shops)

Fig. 2.9: Results of using ME-predicted Scores

comment analysis (ME + twinGraph) can improve system performance for both products and shops ranking.

Algorithm Convergency Verification. Here, we test the algorithm convergency with different settings of Υ and δ that are defined in Section 2.4. Figures 2.10(a)–2.10(c) show the convergency for twinGraph and two

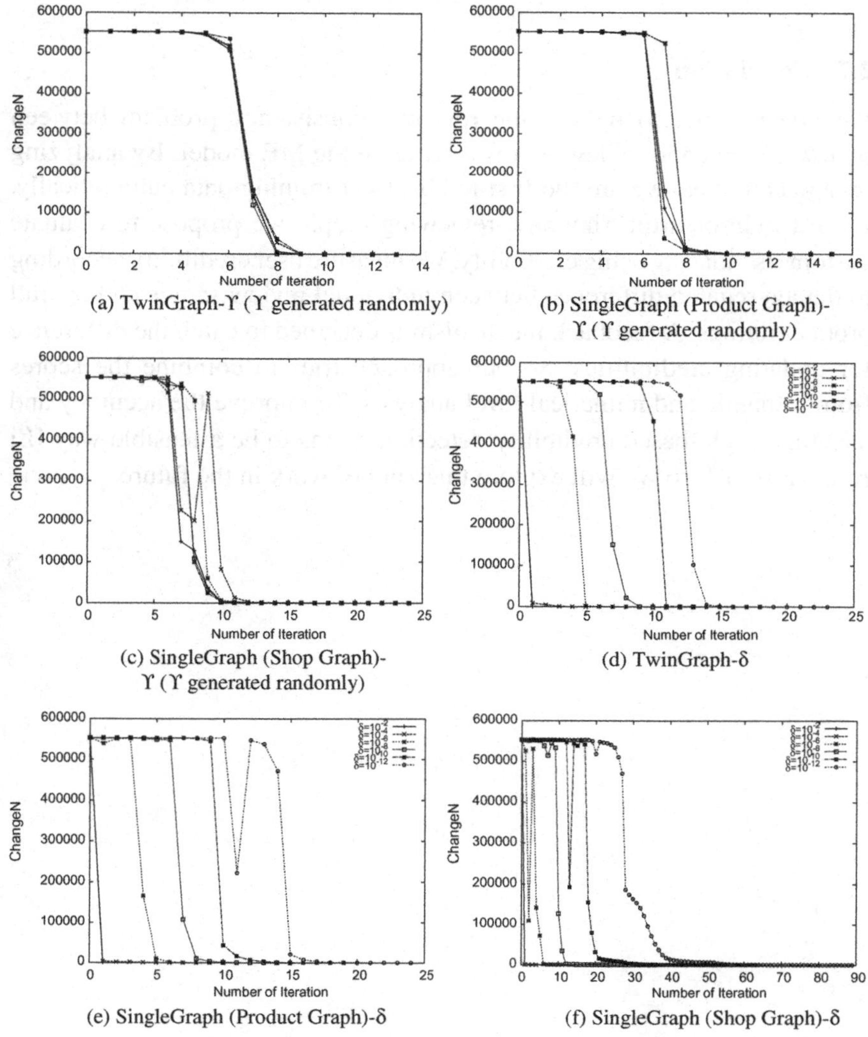

(a) TwinGraph-Υ (Υ generated randomly)

(b) SingleGraph (Product Graph)-Υ (Υ generated randomly)

(c) SingleGraph (Shop Graph)-Υ (Υ generated randomly)

(d) TwinGraph-δ

(e) SingleGraph (Product Graph)-δ

(f) SingleGraph (Shop Graph)-δ

Fig. 2.10: Algorithm Convergency

SingleGraphs with different initial values for Υ, where the initial values for Υ are generated randomly under the range of [0, 1]. We find that all of them have convergency and the convergency paces are almost the same. Each group of experiments reach almost the same credibility distribution for customers. In Figs. 2.10(d)–2.10(f), we test the influence of convergence control parameter δ. We find that the δ can control the convergency speed, and the smaller the δ value, the slower the convergency speed.

2.7 Conclusion

We first propose to resolve the review inconsistency problem between review content and review scores relying on the ME model. By analyzing review activities, we are the first to construct training data automatically. Over a twin-bipartite shopping-reviewing graph, we propose to evaluate customers' honesty using credibility. We measure user credibility according to the aggregated difference between individual review scores and overall product ratings. A feedback mechanism is designed to catch the difference for updating credibilities. So our approach tries to combine the scores from semantic and numerical level analysis. To improve the accuracy and usability, topic-based credibility detection seems to be a feasible way [Li *et al.* (2014a)], so we will explore this kind of work in the future.

Chapter 3

Entity Resolution

Online retailing has been rapidly developed in the past few years, especially on customer-to-customer (C2C) platforms. The explosive growth of products and user-generated content (UGC) such as comments and product description, in both variety and quantity, is an obvious evidence for the booming of C2C E-commerce. Meanwhile, without global supervision on products, the increasing number of C2C websites and involving of large size of vendors lead to an extreme low data quality. One of the major tasks for product management is entity resolution to support efficient services.

Entity resolution has been a basic problem of data integration for decades. However, it meets new challenges dealing with massive sets of web data. We propose two approaches to solve the entity resolution problem for product management. The first one focuses on improving the matching quality using machine learning methods on centralized system, and the second one aims to boost the processing speed on distributed system while dealing with enormous datasets.

3.1 Problem Definition

Entity resolution, also known as entity matching, aims to identify entities that represent the same real-world items. We propose two approaches to enable data integration in this chapter and we formalize our entity resolution problems in this section.

Given a set of entities R, our task is to find out all the entity pairs that are similar to each other in set R. We define that two entities are similar when their similarity is above a certain threshold. There are different metrics that can be used to calculate similarity. For example, Jaccard Similarity is suitable for computing the similarity between two sets and the cosine similarity calculates the similarity between term vectors. Since the given entities consist of either structured or semi-structured and unstructured data, which do not meet the input requirement for the similarity calculation, a batch of data preprocessing steps are needed before computing the similarity. Data preprocessing for structured and unstructured data is different.

- **Schema Integration:** Schema integration is applied to structured entities, which merges different schemas into a global one. It conducts schema fusion to resolve the heterogeneity problems including synonyms, abbreviations, and so on. It also addresses the missing and incorrect data issues. After that, we get the clean data with an uniform schema, then it is suitable to apply the set similarity metrics on them.
- **Tokenization:** For the unstructured content, there is no global schema. So, we tokenize the document-like entities, pick up all meaningful tokens and therefore generate a high-dimensional feature vector for each unstructured entity. Then, we are able to apply cosine similarity on those vectors to figure out the similar pairs.

Definition 3.1 (Similarity Threshold). Similarity threshold θ ($0 \leq \theta \leq 1$) determines the lower bound for generating similar pairs. After the similarity calculation step, those pairs with similarity higher than θ is regarded to be the similar pairs.

Definition 3.2 (Similar Pairs). The set of similar pairs is the result for entity resolution. Entities in the same set refer to the same real-world object. Then, those duplicated records will be eliminated or fused.

In this chapter, we present two frameworks for entity resolution which show different focuses. In Section 3.2, we propose a general learning-based framework for entity resolution based on the centralized system, including data preprocessing, schema integration, value cleaning and entity resolution with logistic regression model. This framework aims at improving the accuracy of entity resolution. It is implemented on centralized system and requires structured data as the input. In Section 3.3, we present a random-based framework on distributed system for entity resolution. It proposes to involve several random algorithms to boost the processing speed of entity resolution on semi-structured and unstructured entities.

3.2 Learning-based Method on Centralized System

In this section, we present a general hybrid framework for entity resolution, which accomplishes entity matching by schema integration and data cleaning. Schema integration aims to provide a uniform and meaningful representation of products. Then, we conduct data cleaning to provide a precise and comprehensive description for each product, which includes missing value filling, incorrect value detection and value confirmation. In our work, schema integration and data cleaning reinforce each other and are the critical steps for the performance of the remaining work. Finally, we employ a logistic regression model to train the similarity threshold among products and cluster products to achieve entity resolution. The framework for entity resolution is shown in Fig. 3.1. The process consists of two parts:

- **Data Preprocessing:** This part first integrates schema by merging different schemas into a global one. Then, it conducts schema fusion to resolve the heterogeneous problems such as synonyms, abbreviation and so on. After that, we address the missing and incorrect data issues. The details will be given in Section 3.2.1.
- **Entity Resolution:** After data preprocessing, we pick features for products and employ logistic regression to learn the product similarity. Finally, products are clustered based on the learned similarity threshold to achieve entity resolution. The details will be given in Section 3.2.2.

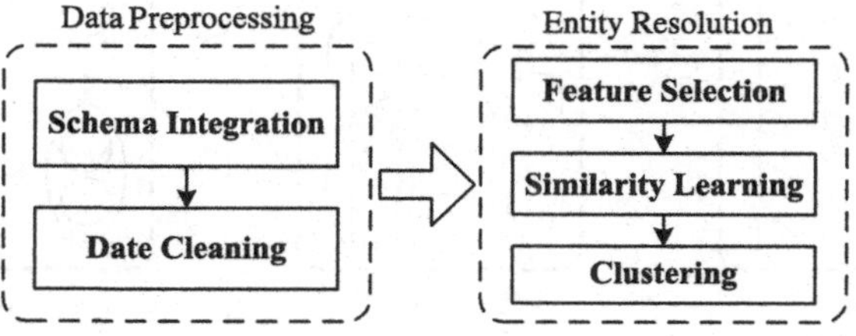

Fig. 3.1: Framework of Learning-based Approach

3.2.1 *Data Preprocessing*

Schema Integration. The usefulness of the attribute table to entity resolution will be negatively affected for lacking of the uniform schema. So, we first integrate the schema, e.g., unifying synonyms and abbreviations. The naive strategy is to merge the strings with high string similarity. This method is not effective, because identical strings may be quite different in the form (e.g., "*RAM*" and "*Random Access Memory*") while strings that are not identical may be quite similar (e.g.,"*Cores Number*" and "*Model Number*").

We take the context-sensitive method to resolve this problem. Our method needs to consider not only string similarity but also the neighbor information called context. To facilitate the remaining work, we first combine attribute tables from all products into a global schema graph $G = \langle A, V, E \rangle$ as shown in Fig. 3.2(a), where A is the set of attributes, V is the set of values and E is the set of edges. For nodes $a \in A$ and $v \in V$, edge (a, v) with weight k exists in G if and only if attribute-value pair (a, v) appears k times in products' attribute tables. The weight of edge (a, v) is represented by $w(a, v)$.

Before grouping similar attributes, we need to merge the identical values (such as "*TL-WR703N*" and "*WR703N*"). Either Edit Distance [Levenshtein (1966)] or N-gram can be used as the similarity measures. We denote the string similarity as $Sim_{Str}(\cdot)$. If values (attributes) combined, it

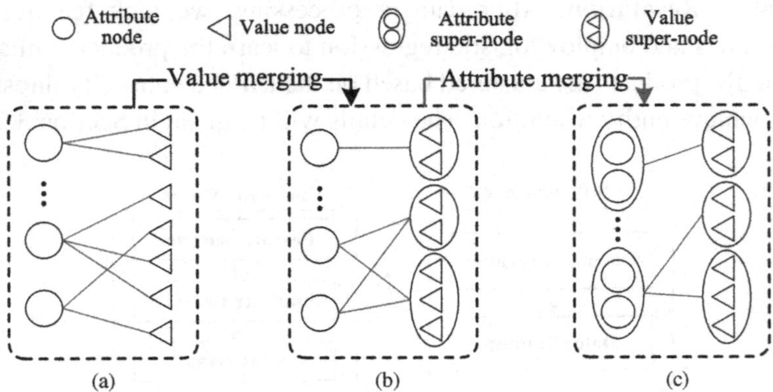

Fig. 3.2: Process of Schema Integration

forms a group of values (attributes) called a value (attribute) super-node as shown in Fig. 3.2. If any two value nodes (value super-nodes) have a higher similarity than a predefined threshold δ ($0 \leq \delta \leq 1$), then we combine them into a super-node. The similarity between a value node a and a super-node v^{sup} is the average similarity between a and nodes in v^{sup}:

$$sim(a, v^{sup}) = \frac{\sum sim(a, a')}{|v^{sup}|}, \quad a' \in v^{sup}.$$

The weight of a super-edge between an attribute a and a value super-node v^{sup} is defined as:

$$w(a, v^{sup}) = \sum_{v \in v^{sup}} w(a, v).$$

After merging, G is converted into $G' = \langle A, V^{sup}, E' \rangle$ as shown in Fig. 3.2(b), where V^{sup} represents the set of value super-nodes and E' represents the set of super-edges. For any value $v \in V$, $sup(v)$ denotes the super-node in V^{sup} which contains v. From any value super-node $v^{sup} \in V^{sup}$, we choose the node appears most frequent in the data pair as the representative, denoted as $v^{sup}.rep$.

Now, we start to merge the identical attributes. As discussed previously, attribute similarity is measured by the string similarity together with the neighbor context similarity. The similarity of any two attributes $a_i, a_j \in A$ is defined as:

$$S_{att}(a_i, a_j) = \lambda Sim_{Str}(a_i, a_j) + (1 - \lambda) S_{neighbor}(a_i, a_j),$$

$$S_{neighbor}(a_i, a_j) = \frac{\sum_{v \in V(a_i) \cap V(a_j)} Min(w(a_i, v), w(a_j, v))}{\sum_{v \in V(a_i) \cup V(a_j)} Max(w(a_i, v), w(a_j, v))},$$

where $S_{att}(\cdot)$ is the weighted sum of string similarity and neighbor context similarity. Here, λ is adjustable. For any $a \in A$, $V(a)$ denotes the set of super-nodes in V^{sup} which are adjacent to a in the graph. Neighbor similarity evaluates the ratio of common values connected with the two attributes a_i and a_j. Using $S_{att}(\cdot)$ and a given threshold θ, with $0 \leq \theta \leq 1$, we merge the attributes according to the same strategy as merging values. After attribute merging, we get $G^* = \langle A^{sup}, V^{sup}, E^* \rangle$ as shown in Fig. 3.2(c). For any attribute super-node $a^{sup} \in A^{sup}$, $a^{sup}.rep$ denotes the representative node in a^{sup}, which is the attribute in a^{sup} that appears the most frequent among the data pairs.

Now, the integrated schema is stored in G^*, where different attributes (values) within a super-node are considered identical. Then, we can use graph G^* to represent all products with a uniform data schema. For each attribute-value pair (a, v) of product p, there may be two super-nodes $a^{sup} \in A^{sup}$ and $v^{sup} \in V^{sup}$ in graph G^* containing a and v respectively. We convert (a, v) to $(a^{sup}.rep, v^{sup}.rep)$. After the conversion, all products are in a unified data schema, so a more accurate comparison based on attribute table can be achieved.

Data Filling and Cleaning. The missing and incorrect values greatly deteriorate the performance for entity resolution. So, now we introduce the methods of data filling and cleaning.

As shown in Fig. 3.3(a), we use a bipartite graph $g^{(p)} = \langle A^{(p)}, V^{(p)}, E^{(p)} \rangle$ to model the attribute table of product p, where $A^{(p)}$ is the set of attributes, $V^{(p)}$ is the set of values, and an edge in $E^{(p)}$ represents an attribute-value pair in p (the original weight for each edge is 1). And we use $tit(p)$ and $des(p)$ to denote title and textual description for product p, respectively.

- Missing value filling: There are two types of missing values:
  - **(i)** *Value-level missing*: An attribute's corresponding value is "*null*", e.g., in Fig. 3.3(a), a_3 is the value-level missing;

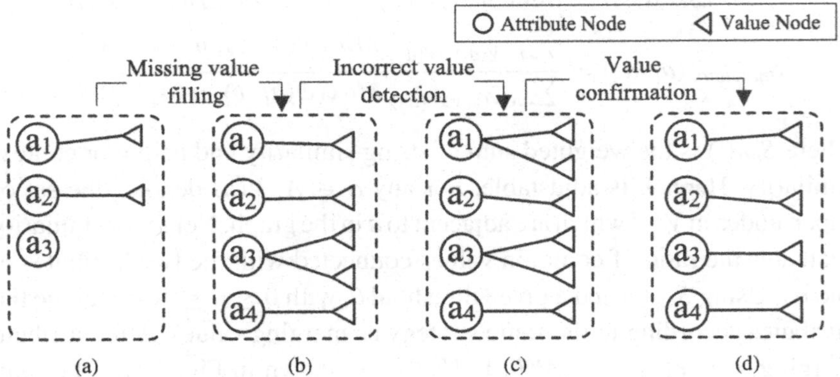

Fig. 3.3: Process of Data Cleaning

Table 3.1: Example of Products' Descriptions

Title	Price	Attribute Table	Textual Description
3G TAX FREE 150M portable Wi-Fi Wireless Router TP-LINK TL-WR703N	\$29.99	Brand: null Model number: TL-WR703N Type: Wireless router Ports number: 4 ports	With a compact form factor, the TP-Link TL-WR703N 150 Mbps Wi-Fi router provides 3G wireless...
TP-LINK 150M Mini wireless router 300M speed iPad3 iPhone5	\$31.99	Brand: TP-Link Max.Rate: 150Mbps Product Model: null	TL-WR703N is small enough to put into your pocket and...
TL-WR703N Mini Wi-Fi wireless router 300M speed	\$31.99	Max.Rate: 150Mbps Product Model: TL-MR3220	TP-link TL-WR703N is a truly plug and play wireless router...

(ii) *Schema-level missing*: It occurs when a product does not have an attribute it should have. In Table 3.1, the third product does not have the attribute "*brand*" which is owned by other similar products.

The process of filling missing values is described in Algorithm 3.1. The first step is to locate those attributes that are either value-level missing or schema-level missing, and store them in A_{miss}. Note that only the representative attribute is stored into A_{miss} to avoid redundancy. For each attribute $a_i \in A_{miss}$, we scan $tit(p)$ and $des(p)$ for any sub-string which is equal to any element $v \in \bigcup_{a \in a_i} V(a)$, and $V(a)$ represents the value for attribute a. If any sub-string is equal to v, then it is considered as the candidate value for a_i. So, we create a new edge (a_i, v) into $g'^{(p)}$ with weight 1, if the edge already exists, we plus 1 to the weight. Based on the result of Algorithm 3.1, we get a new bipartite graph $g'^{(p)} = \langle A'^{(p)}, V'^{(p)}, E'^{(p)} \rangle$, which has some new nodes and new edges compared with $g^{(p)}$, as shown in Fig. 3.3(b). New attribute nodes in $A'^{(g)}$ are evidences found for schema-level missing, and new value nodes in $V'^{(p)}$ are candidates found for value-level missing. The weights of new edges in $E'^{(p)}$ are the support degree of evidences found from $tit(p)$ and $des(p)$. For any new attribute nodes in $g'^{(p)}$ which connect to two or

Algorithm 3.1 Missing Data Filling

Input: $G^* = \langle A^{sup}, V^{sup}, E^* \rangle, tit(p), des(p),$
$g^{(p)} = \langle A^{(p)}, V^{(p)}, E^{(p)} \rangle$
Output: $g'^{(p)}$

$V_{miss} = \emptyset, g'^{(p)} = g^{(p)}$
for each $a_i \in A^{sup}$ **do**
  if $a_i.rep \notin A^{(p)}$ *or* $(a_i.rep, null) \in E^{(p)}$ **then**
    $A_{miss} \leftarrow a_i.rep$
  end if
end for
for each $a_i \in A_{miss}$ **do**
  for each $v \in \bigcup_{a \in a_i} V(a)$ **do**
    if v appears in $tit(p)$ or $des(p)$ **then**
      if $(a_i, sup(v).rep) \in E^{(p)}$ **then**
        $w(a_i, sup(v).rep) = w(a_i, sup(v).rep) + 1$
      else
        $E'^{(p)} \leftarrow (a_i, sup(v).rep)$
        $w(a_i, sup(v).rep) = 1$
      end if
    end if
  end for
end for
return $g'^{(p)}$

more nodes such as a_3 in Fig. 3.3(b), we need to determine which value node is the right one. The process will be described in the part of value confirmation.

- Incorrect value detection: For product p, the incorrect value can be deduced from $tit(p)$ or $des(p)$. For example, for the third product in Table 3.1, the title and textual description imply that the true value for "*Product Model*" should be "*TL-WR703N*". Algorithm 3.2 shows the process for incorrect value detection. For each attribute $a_i \in A^{(p)}$, we check whether the current value for a_i may be improper by using the sub-string in $tit(p)$ or $des(p)$. If there is such a sub-string, we remove the edge, reduce the weight by one correspondingly.

Algorithm 3.2 Incorrect Value Detection

Input: $G^* = \langle A^{sup}, V^{sup}, E^* \rangle, tit(p), des(p),$
$g'^{(p)} = \langle A'^{(p)}, V'^{(p)}, E'^{(p)} \rangle, A^{(p)}$

Output: $g'^{(p)}$

for each $a_i \in A^{(p)}$ **do**
    for each $v \in \cup_{a \in a_i} V(a)$ **do**
        if v appears in $tit(p)$ or $des(p)$ **then**
            if $\langle a_i, sup(v).rep \rangle \in E'^{(p)}$ **then**
                $w(a_i, sup(v).rep) = w(a_i, sup(v).rep) + 1$
            else
                $g'^{(p)} \leftarrow (a_i, sup(v).rep)$
                $w(a_i, sup(v).rep) = 1$
            end if
        end if
    end for
end for
return $g'^{(p)}$

- Value confirmation: After missing value filling and incorrect value detection, the graph $g'^{(p)}$ for product p may contain some multi-valued attributes which connect to more than one values, such as a_1 and a_3 in Fig. 3.3(c). We should decide which value is the right one.

  For any $a_i \in A'^{(p)}$, we denote $V'^{(p)}(a_i)$ to be the set of value nodes that connect to a_i. For each attribute node $a_i \in A'^{(p)}$ that connects to two or more value nodes, we choose one from all the value nodes connected to a_i according to the following two criteria:

(1) $v = argmax_{v \in V'^{(p)}(a)} w(a_i, v)$.

$$(2)\ \ v = \begin{cases} original\ value & \text{if } \dfrac{max\, w(a_i, v)}{\sum_{v \in V'^{(p)}(a)} w(a_i, v)} < \gamma \\ argmax_{v \in V'^{(p)}(a)} w(a_i, v) & \text{otherwise.} \end{cases}$$

The first criterion is straightforward, which selects the value with the maximum weight. The second criterion is more passive. It chooses the value with the maximum weight only if the maximum weight exceeds a percentage (a threshold γ) of total weights. Otherwise, we keep the original value to avoid incorrect "repair" of the right value. γ is between [0, 1].

After removing the contradicted values in $g'^{(p)}$, we obtain a new graph as shown in Fig. 3.3(d), where the missing data is filled and the incorrect value is repaired.

3.2.2 *Entity Resolution*

After data preprocessing is done by unifying attribute table from the view of schema and value, we now use the integrated data for entity resolution.

Product Feature Selection. We pick the features and define the similarity measurement for each feature.

Attribute table contains the standard features for product discriminating because it is detailed and more focused, especially after schema integration and data cleaning. We use every attribute node in G^* as a feature, and we get $|A^{sup}|$ features. The similarity between two products on the ith feature is defined as:

$$s_i(value_k, value_j) = \begin{cases} 1 & \text{if } value_k = value_j \\ 0 & \text{otherwise.} \end{cases}$$

Title is another important feature. Sellers often add popular but irrelevant keywords to titles. We use word segmentation tools to partition t_i and t_j into two sets of words $w(t_i)$ and $w(t_j)$, and use *tf–idf* to give a less weight to these irrelative words, then the similarity between two titles is:

$$Sim_{title}(t_i, t_j) = \frac{\sum_{w \in w(t_i) \cap w(t_j)} tf(w) \times idf(w)}{\sum_{w \in w(t_i) \cup w(t_j)} tf(w) \times idf(w)}.$$

Price is important feature for entity resolution, because a considerable differ in price between two products may give evidence that they refer to two different entities. The price similarity is defined as:

$$Sim_{price}(price_i, price_j) = 1 - \frac{|price_i - price_j|}{max\,(price_i, price_j)}.$$

Online review is also an important feature. We observe that reviews for the similar products are always involved in many common aspects.

To extract feature from reviews, we use word segmentation and POS tagging tool [Zhang *et al.* (2003)] to partition sentences in reviews into words and POS tags, and extract nouns as aspect words. Many aspect words such as "*quality*" and "*shipping*" are not discriminative since they appear frequently in many products. So, we use *tf–idf* to score every aspect word and pick the top k aspect words. We use $Asp(p) = \{w_1, \ldots, w_k\}$ to denote the top k aspect words of product p. The similarity of two products on the feature of reviews is:

$$Sim_{reviews}(p_i, p_j) = \frac{|Asp(p_i) \cap Asp(p_j)|}{|Asp(p_i) \cup Asp(p_j)|}.$$

Model Training. Now for any product, we have $k = |A^{sup} + 3|$ features with $|A^{sup}|$ features in attribute table, and three features in title, price and reviews respectively. Using the predefined similarity functions, we can obtain a similarity vector $\mathbf{s}(p_i, p_j) = \langle s_1, \ldots, s_k \rangle$ for products p_i and p_j. We convert the problem of whether two products are matching, to be two-class classification problem, and use linear logistic regression model to do classification.

The reason for using two-classification instead of multi-class classification is twofold:

(i) The number of parameters for two-classification is much smaller than multi-class classification, especially when the entity number is large.
(ii) In multi-class classification, the training set must cover all classes, which is difficult because entity number is usually either too large or not known.

We set C_0 to be matching and C_1 to be mismatching. The posterior probability of class C_0 can be modeled as logistic sigmoid acting on a linear function of the feature vector **s** so that:

$$p(C_0|s) = y(\mathbf{s}) = \frac{1}{1 + e^{-\mathbf{w}^T\mathbf{s}}} = \frac{1}{1 + e^{-(w^T s + w_0)}},$$

where w_0 is a bias and $\mathbf{w}$ is the weight vector for features, and $\mathbf{s} = [1, \underline{s}]$.

We use training data to train **w** so that $\mathbf{w}^T \underline{\mathbf{s}} > 0$ is for matching and $\mathbf{w}^T \mathbf{s} < 0$ is for mismatching. After the training, the kth value in w indicates the importance of the kth feature in the discriminative function.

Entity Resolution via Clustering. After we trained a model for the probability of two products' matching, we need to convert pairwise matching into partitions so that products in each partition refer to a unique underlying entity. The naive way is to generate a graph where nodes represent products and there is an edge between two nodes if and only if the probability of two products' matching is more than 0.5. However, this method will cause low precision since an incorrect prediction of matching will merge two partitions by mistake.

Our solution is to treat the probability of two products' matching as similarity, then apply clustering algorithm to partition. This solution is effective since clustering makes global decision rather than local decision. For n products, we can get a similarity matrix $\mathbf{M}_{n \times n}$ where m_{ij} is the similarity (estimated probability of matching) between product i and j. We use existing cluster algorithm such as the hierarchical Aggregation Cluster (HAC) or k-means to partition products into clusters. The number of clusters is determined in the process of clustering according to the purity or diameter. When n is large, the cost for both storage and computation is very large. Our solution is to use taxonomy information to divide the n products into several disjoin subsets so that each subset is a separate category with smaller number of products.

3.3 Random-based Method on Distributed System

As the data increases, distributed data processing is an optimal way to increase resolution usability. In this section, we propose a random-based matching algorithm for semi-structured and unstructured data on MapReduce framework, which is a distributed framework for entity resolution. Our method expects to reduce both the computation cost and network transmission cost during entity resolution and therefore get a boost on processing speed. In order to promise a good match accuracy for high dimensional data points, entity matching in our framework is expected to solve the following problems: *entity similarity calculation*, *candidate entity pair generation* and *implementation on MapReduce*.

3.3.1 *Framework Introduction*

In our random-based entity matching framework, we aim at solving the entity matching problem on semi-structured and unstructured data. After tokenizing the input data and generating high-dimensional feature vectors based on the words frequency, we obtain a set of high dimensional vectors representing entity features. We use these vectors as system input. The goal is to find all matching pairs among these entity vectors. We define that two entities are matched when their similarity distance is lower than a predefined threshold.

Figure 3.4 shows matching framework on MapReduce. Before doing the matching process, we carry out three steps of preprocessing on the source data to get our expected input. Initially, we split the input entities into tokens using the Part-of-Speech Tagger [Toutanova *et al.* (2003)]. Then, we generate a dictionary containing all k different tokens occurred in the dataset. Finally, for each entity u, a k-dimension vector V_u is generated, in which the nth dimension represent the word frequency of the nth token in entity u. The input of our method is a set of (*key*, *value*) pairs made up of entity ID E_u and its k-dimension vector V_u. In addition, another standard vector set R is introduced into the MapReduce job, which contains d ($d \ll k$) numbers of k bits random vectors of unit length, i.e., $\{r_1, r_2, \ldots, r_d\}$. By using both the original data vectors and the R set, we generate for each vector a d-dimensional signature. We produce candidate

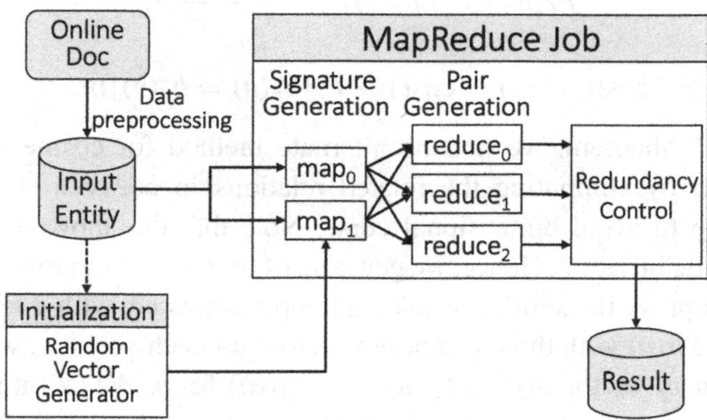

Fig. 3.4: Framework of Random-based Approach

pairs from these signatures. Additionally, in order to reduce redundance computing, we spend one more round of MapReduce for reduce removing.

3.3.2 *Entity Signature Generation*

For processing semi-structured and unstructured entities, cosine similarity is a suitable method. However, it faces the high dimensional entity features which definitely reduces match accuracy. A low dimension conversion is needed. Additionally, for data shuffle, high dimensional data transmission will consume a large part of network. In order to tackle with the problems mentioned above, we propose a new framework for entity resolution based on Locality Sensitive Hashing (LSH) [Charikar (2002)] implemented on MapReduce.

$$h_r(u) = \begin{cases} 1, & r \cdot u \geq 0 \\ 0, & r \cdot u < 0. \end{cases} \tag{3.1}$$

Theorem. Suppose we have a collection of vectors in a k dimensional vector space N^k. Then, we generate a random vector r of unit length from this k dimensional space. We define a hash function h_r as Equation (3.1). For any vectors u and v, we can achieve the similarity probability by Equation (3.2). It has been proved by Goemans and Williamson (1995). Then, we can get the cosine relationship for any pair of vectors (u, v) as expressed in Equation (3.3).

$$Pr[h_r(u) = h_r(v)] = 1 - \frac{\theta(u, v)}{\pi}, \tag{3.2}$$

$$\cos(\theta(u, v)) = \cos(1 - Pr[h_r(u) = h_r(v)])\pi. \tag{3.3}$$

By this theorem, we find an alternate method for cosine similarity calculation by computing the related relationship between vectors and it can help to avoid dimensional curse. Note that the above equation is probabilistic in nature. Hence, we generate (d) number of random vectors to achieve improve the similarity calculation performance, with $d \ll k$. After calculating $h(u)$ with those d random vectors for each vector u, we can get a d-bit binary vector $(h_1(u), h_2(u), \ldots, h_d(u))$ for u. We call it signature $S_d(u)$ for vector u. Since the signature maintains characteristics of the vector, the huge deviation between two signatures means these two vectors differ a lot. Applying Equation (3.3), we get cosine similarity between any two vectors. Moreover, as we increase d to expand the signature, it will give more accurate results for similarity calculation.

On the other hand, it is observed that $Pr[h_r(u) = h_r(v)] = 1 - (hamming\ distance)/d$. Thus, it converts the problem of finding cosine similarity between vectors to the problem of finding hamming distance between signatures. It provides us a faster and highly memory efficient option for similarity calculation. In such a way, we reduce a vector in high k dimensional space to that of d dimensional bool space whilst it still preserves cosine similarity, where $d \ll k$. In the following descriptions, hamming distance has the same meaning as cosine similarity.

3.3.3 *Candidate Pair Generation*

Similar entities often have similar signatures. An extreme example is, if two entities are the same, they share the same signature. However, if we sort a set of signatures directly, all of those similar entity pairs may not be close by their hamming distance. This is highly decided by the signature generation process. For instance, no matter how similar the two signatures are, the results of their lexicographically sort may differ a lot if they have a difference in the first bit of their signatures. In order to tackle this problem, we propose to do random permutation for these signatures as proposed by Point Location in Equal Balls (PLEB), which was first mentioned by Indyk and Motwani (1998) and improved by Charikar (2002). This algorithm takes random permutations to signatures and sorts the permutated signatures. It aims to find vectors with short hamming distances.

After generating different kinds of permutations, signature pairs with lower hamming distance may have higher possibility to get closer in some of their sorting results. Therefore, we can find the m number of closest neighbors for each signature $S_d(u)$ and then generate entity pairs for u. Implementation details can be found in the following part.

Matching Framework on MapReduce. We aim at solving the entity matching problem on semi-structured and unstructured data. We preprocess the input data by tokenizing and normalizing them. For each item u, we generate its feature vector based on the term frequency. We use those high-dimensional vectors as our data input. Our goal is to find all entity pairs that

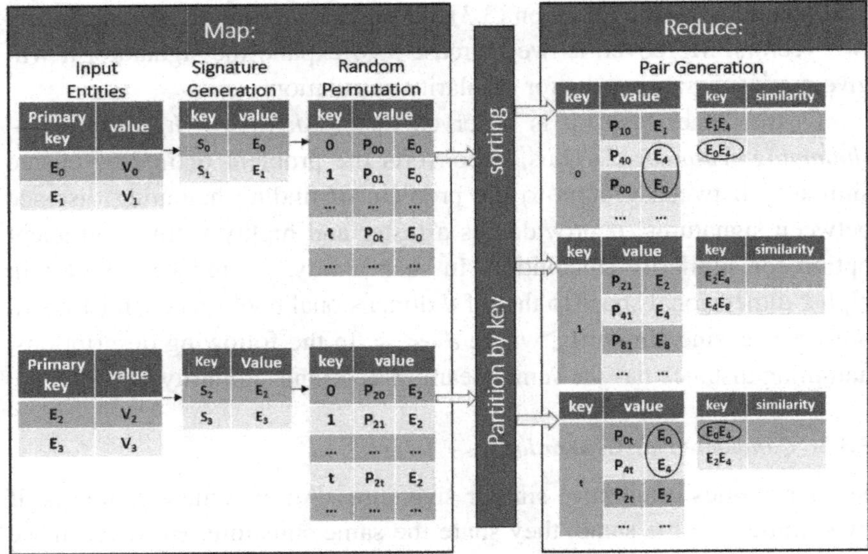

Fig. 3.5: An Example of Matching via MapReduce

are matched. Two entities are matched when their hamming distance on the signatures is lower than a predefined threshold. We can get the output from the top N similar pairs by an additional sorting process on the result set.

3.3.3.1 *Implementation on MapReduce*

Figure 3.5 illustrates the processing workflow of MapReduce job. Map phase contains steps as following:

(1) Initially, we apply $h_r(u)$ to each input entity (E_u, V_u) using R as the standard vector set. We pair V_u with every vector r_i in R $(1 \leq i \leq d)$ and calculate $h_{ri}(u)$, then we get a d-bit binary signature S_u for V_u represented as: $\overline{S_u} = \{h_{r1}(u), h_{r2}(u), \ldots, h_{rd}(u)\}$.

(2) After converting the input vectors into signatures S_u, we randomly permute them t times. The permutation function can be approximated as:

$$\pi(x) = (ax + b)\ mod\ p, \tag{3.4}$$

where p is prime and $0 < a < p$, $0 \leq b < p$. Both a and b are chosen randomly. We apply t different random permutation for every signature (by choosing random values for a and b, t number of times). Thus for each signature S_u, we have t different permutation results: $\{P_{u1}, P_{u2}, \ldots, P_{ut}\}$. We regard this result as our map output. As a consequence, we have t different map output for each entity represented as (i, P_{ui}, E_u), with i, P_{ui} and E_u referring permutation number, the corresponding permutation result and the entity ID.

In reduce phase, we expect to achieve entity pair similarity. After an automatic sorting procedure during the shuffle between map and reduce, the reduce phase faces t number of groups represented as (i, L_i), in which L_i is the sorted list on all signatures in the ith round of permutation. Then, we generate matching pairs between every entity u and its closest m neighbors in the sorted list. Finally, we calculate the hamming distance of every paired entities and output those with distance below a predefined threshold. The output is formatted as $(E_u E_v, \mathit{similarity})(u < v)$ which are the ID concatenation of paired entities' with its similarity value.

Overall, the map tasks change each k-dimension vector into t number of d-bit signatures. d and t are always far less than k. Generally, d and t are between tens to hundreds while k are normally more than tens of thousands determined by the characteristic and size of input data. That gives a significant reduction on data volume, and also a huge cut on the network transmission cost between map and reduce. Unlike most of the blocking-based entity matching methods comprised by multiple MapReduce tasks, our matching algorithm is finished in one MapReduce job. Since each MapReduce task spends extra cost on task scheduling and network communication, the cutting on the number of MapReduce jobs can lead to performance promotion. Since all permutations of any signature are sent to reducers by the permutation number i, each reduce will then have the same number of pairs and may not have the load skew problem.

3.3.4 *Redundancy Reduction*

For different groups in one reduce tasks, there can be many duplication matching pairs. It is to say the same pair $(E_u \cdot E_v)$ may be generated by both group a and group b, and it may cause a redundant computation and waste a lot of time. For example, in Fig. 3.5, there are two duplicate pairs

(E_0E_4) and (E_2E_4) in reduce output. It is a pervasive problem in many MapReduce-based matching algorithms. The reason for the occurrence of these redundancies is that, the features of one entity are separated into multiple parts during the map phase, and each part of this entity may possibly match any part of the another entity in the reduce phase. It may happen more frequently on the entity pairs with higher similarity, because of the higher possibility for each feature part to be matched.

Several works have been done to solve this problem. In redundancy-free similarity computation model [Kolb *et al.* (2013)], it adds additional annotate on each map output to tell reducers which the rest parts of this entity will be sent to. Though it is efficient, it bases on a strong precondition that all entities sent to the same reducer will definitely be paired among each other. In our algorithm, the permuted signatures of the same entity is sent to all reducers, and for each reducer, a signature is only paired with its neighborhoods. So this redundancy-free solution is not suitable for our random-based method.

We introduce an extra MapReduce job to reduce duplication. Figure 3.6 shows an example of our method. We modify the original MapReduce job in the reduce phase by cutting off the similarity computation step. After generating all pairs, the reduce task terminates and outputs those pairwise information with entity IDs E_u *and* E_v $(u < v)$ as *key* and their t^{th} permuted signature P_{ut} *and* P_{vt} as *values*, that is $(E_uE_v, P_{ut}P_{vt})$.

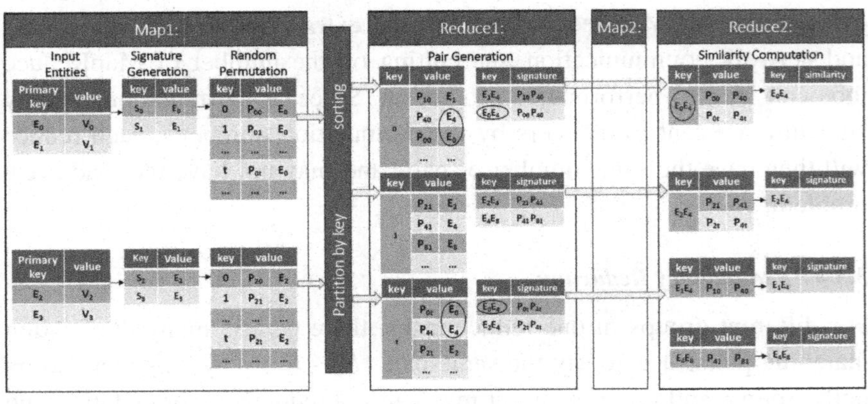

Fig. 3.6: An Example of Deduplication

The map phase of the second MapReduce job is an identity mapper which does nothing during the map phase. In the following shuffle phase, all pairs with the same entity IDs are grouped together. It means that all those duplicated pairs come together. It looks like $(E_u E_v, list(P_{u1} P_{v1}, P_{u4} P_{v4}, \ldots, P_{ut} P_{vt}))$ as the input for reduce phase, so the only thing we need to do is to pick one pair of permuted signatures to calculate hamming distance. The hamming distance for every pair of permuted signatures is the same in the list. Finally, we output the similarity $(E_u E_v, similarity)$ as our result.

3.4 Experimental Results

In this section, we describe the details of our experiments. Then, we show the experimental results for these two different entity resolution frameworks separately.

3.4.1 *Results of Learning-based Method*

Dataset. The dataset is crawled from Taobao, the largest E-commerce site. The dataset covers 168 categories, over 1,400,000 products, 500,000 sellers and 78,000,000 reviews. We choose 12 representative categories, and randomly sample 15% products for experiments as shown in Table 3.2. We also produce the statistics for noise in our dataset.

Noise in titles: We denote the noise by the percentage of irrelevant words in titles. Word that cannot indicate what entity the product refers to is called an irrelevant word (e.g., advertising words such as "*excellent*",

Table 3.2: Categories of Dataset

Categories	#.of Products	#.of Entities	Categories	#.of Products	#.of Entities
Phone	5,345	98	Wallet and purse	2,090	108
Camera	8,980	89	Jacket	3,334	79
Notebook	5,879	168	perfume	1,090	67
Network devices	12,324	127	Shampoo	2,073	103
T-shirt	8,977	333	Women's shoes	3,909	159
Jeans	9,006	206	Sport shoes	6,348	298

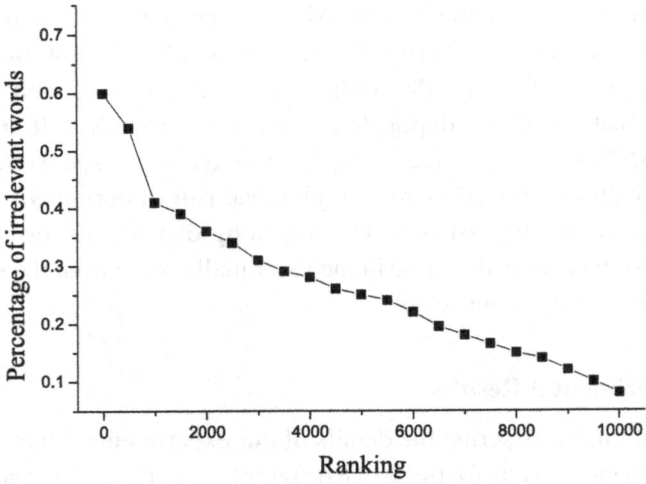

Fig. 3.7: Percentage of Non-relative Words in Titles

"*free Tax*", etc. and misleading words such as "*iPad3*" for a router). Irrelevant words are noise for entity resolution. We randomly choose 1,000 products from our dataset and manually label irrelevant words in their titles. Figure 3.7 shows the percentage of irrelevant words (items are ranked in descending order of the percentage). It is surprising that over 30% titles have at least 30% irrelevant words, and over 80% titles have at least 15% irrelevant words. Due to the noise, the performance of entity resolution that only uses title is extremely low as shown in Fig. 3.9.

Noise in attribute table: To evaluate the noise in attribute table, we randomly sample 1,000 products and manually label missing and incorrect values, then calculate the number of null values and incorrect values respectively for each product. The result is shown in Fig. 3.8 (products are ranked in descending order according to the percentage respectively). The surprising result shows that 90% products have data quality problems in their attribute tables, and data quality is severely low for 50% products.

Evaluation on Data Cleaning. We use our data cleaning algorithm to fill the missing values and repair the incorrect values on the 1,000 products we have labeled with the prudent parameter γ to be 0, 0.2 and 0.4 respectively, then evaluate the accuracy and recall. The results are shown in Table 3.3.

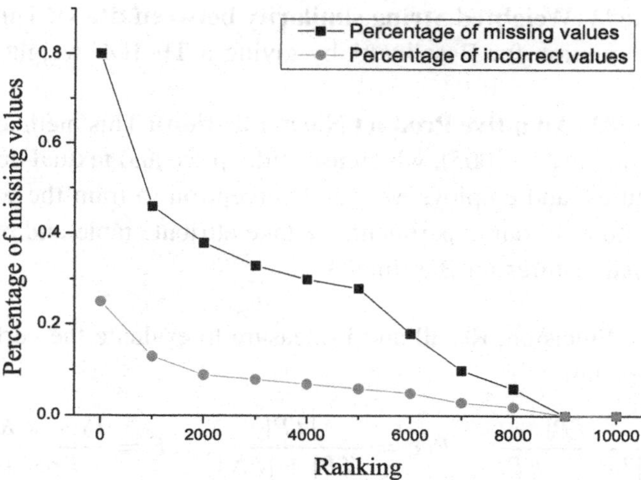

Fig. 3.8: Percentage of Missing and Incorrect Values in Attribute Table

Table 3.3: Precision and Recall of Data Cleaning

	Missing Values Filling		Incorrect Values Repair	
	Precision	Recall	Precision	Recall
$\gamma = 0$	0.85	0.78	0.72	0.75
$\gamma = 0.2$	**0.95**	**0.75**	**0.92**	**0.65**
$\gamma = 0.4$	0.98	0.43	0.93	0.25

The results show that our data cleaning algorithm wins a high precision and recall, especially when $\gamma = 0.2$ (the rest of our experiments use this setting). Note that the precision is more important than the recall in our scenario, because a mistaken value filling (repair) is serious, while leaving some missing (incorrect) values unfilled (unrepaired) is acceptable.

Evaluation on Entity Resolution. This subsection will compare the effectiveness of our framework with three Baselines:

- **Baseline#1 (String similarity between titles):** This method just uses String similarity on titles. Two products are considered to be matching if the similarity is over the threshold η.

- **Baseline#2 (Weighted String similarity between titles):** This method is a melioration for Baseline#1 by giving a TF–IDF weight for each word.
- **Baseline#3 (Adaptive Product Normalization):** This method is based on Bilenko *et al.* (2005), which uses title, price and textual description for features, and employs averaged perceptron to train the weight for each feature. In our experiment, we take attribute table and reviews as additional features for Baseline#3.

We use Precision, Recall and F-measure to evaluate the performance of entity resolution:

$$Prec = \frac{|TP|}{|TP| + |FP|}, \quad Rec = \frac{|TP|}{|TP| + |FN|}, \quad F = \frac{Prec \times Rec \times 2}{Prec + Rec},$$

where $|TP|$, $|FP|$ and $|FN|$ are the numbers of true positive, false positive and false negative respectively.

We ran the three Baseline approaches and our approach on the 12 categories respectively. For Baseline#1 and Baseline#2, there is no model needed to train. The threshold η is the tradeoff parameter for Precision and Recall.

Figure 3.9 shows the average Precision, Recall and F-measure score of the 12 categories. It is clear that the performance of Baseline#1 and Baseline#2 are very low. We found that the Recall value is almost 0 when the Precision is high. That is because when we set the threshold η too high, Baseline#1 and Baseline#2 will only predict products with the same titles to be matching. Note that the Precision drops significantly when we increase the recall requirement. It is because the titles of many different products are similar due to the high rate of irrelevant words. Baseline#2 is better than Baseline#1, because we give a less weight to irrelevant words. However, due to the existence of noise in titles, the performance of these approaches are very low.

Baseline#3 is much better than the two approaches. That is because Baseline#3 uses more features and employ a machine learning method to train the weight for each feature. Compared with Baseline#3, our approach is better. The reason is twofold: (i) We integrate schema so that the attribute table can be used much more efficiently, since the identical attributes with

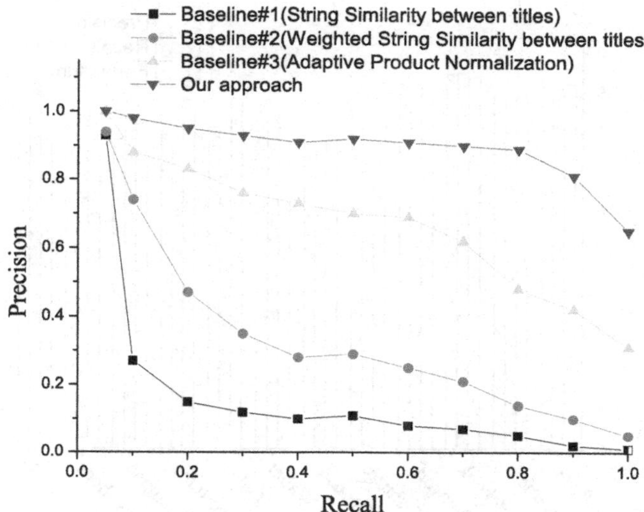

Fig. 3.9: Performance Comparison Between Baselines and Ours

different expressions can be traded as the same one. (ii) We fill the missing values and repair the incorrect values.

To show the importance of our schema integration and data cleaning for entity resolution, we defined three variants of our approach: *complete approach*, *without data cleaning*, *neither schema integration nor data cleaning*.

We ran experiments on these three kinds of settings in each category respectively. Figure 3.10 shows the F-measure scores. It shows that with the help of schema integration, the performance is improved in all categories, which validates the role of Schema Integration. After data cleaning, the F-measure is improved significantly in all categories, which validates the need of data cleaning for entity resolution in C2C sites and the effectiveness of our data cleaning method.

3.4.2 *Results of Random-based Method*

We run experiments on a 22-node HP blade cluster. Each node has two Intel Xeon processors E5335 2.00GHz with four cores and one thread per core, 16GB of RAM, and two 1TB hard disks. All nodes run in CentOS 6.5, Hadoop 1.2.1 and Java 1.7.0. In this section, we evaluate the performance

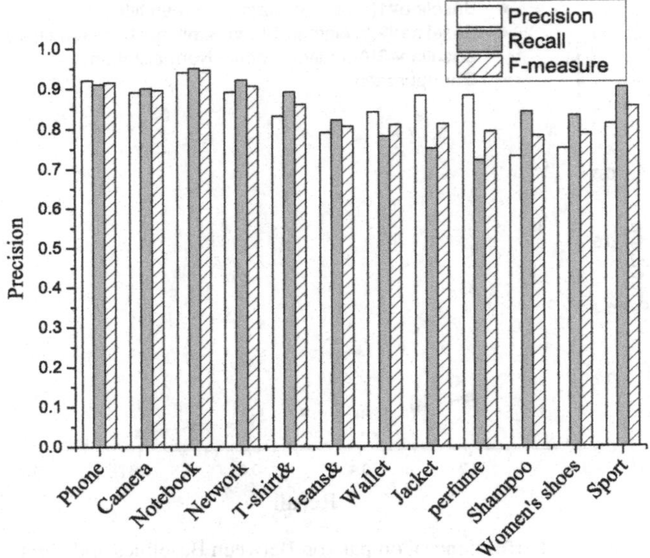

Fig. 3.10: Performance of Three Variant Approaches

of our random-based matching algorithm in two aspects: (1) We measure the effect on performance and quality by selecting different parameters. (2) We compare the performance of our algorithms with the state-of-the-art matching algorithm namely Document Similarity Self-Join (DSSJ) [Baraglia *et al.* (2010)] and Dedoop [Kolb *et al.* (2012a)].

Dataset. We run experiments on the CiteSeerX dataset. It contains nearly 1.32 Million citations of total size 2.89 GB in XML format. Each citation includes *record ID, author, title, date, page, volume, publisher, etc.* and also a document attribute, *abstract*. We retain all the attributes for verification as we consider all those information are useful and our matching results can benefit from it. In addition, we select a few records from CiteseerX and manually make validation sets for accuracy evaluation.

Evaluation on Parameter Selection. There are three parameters that may affect the performance:

- *d*: The length of the signature. It directly determines the network transmission cost and accuracy. A bigger *d* leads to a longer signature, and therefore increases the burden of network transmission, but it can benefit the accuracy since the signature may contain more information of the entity.

- t: The number of permutations. It multiplies the data transmission between map and reduce. The increase of t can also raise the pair redundancy and increase the run-time, but improve the matching accuracy.
- m: The window of selecting neighborhoods. It decides the amount of pairs and also causes a change on redundancy ratio. It can influence the result accuracy and execution time as well.

We introduce four metrics to evaluate system performance:

- The **network transmission cost** is measured by summing up the size of map output since all output of map phase will be sent to reducers through network.
- The **run-time** of MapReduce jobs is recorded to compare the speed of our algorithm with different parameters.
- The **redundancy rate** is calculated as total number of generated pairs/distinct candidate pairs to show the redundancy ratio.
- The **accuracy** is also measured in this part. In order to calculate the accuracy, we prepare a validation set which contains 200 entity records for accuracy measurement. We calculate the similarity between those entities manually and generate a set of top 50 similar entity pairs as the standard result set. The accuracy is measured as the fraction of pairs that appear within the standard top 50 results.

To evaluate the performance, we first use a 200MB subset of CiteSeerX as our input to the effect of changing parameters. Figures 3.11–3.16 show the performance variations of our algorithm when changing one of the three parameters. Figures 3.11, 3.13 and 3.15 illustrate the run-time for both of two MapReduce jobs with MR1 for pair generation and MR2 for deduplication, and the transmission cost during MapReduce tasks. We can see from Fig. 3.11 that when we increase the length of signature d, the network transmission cost together with the run-time of MapReduce jobs has a steady growth. Meanwhile, in Fig. 3.12, as the increasing of d, the redundancy decreases steadily and the accuracy increases smoothly. The

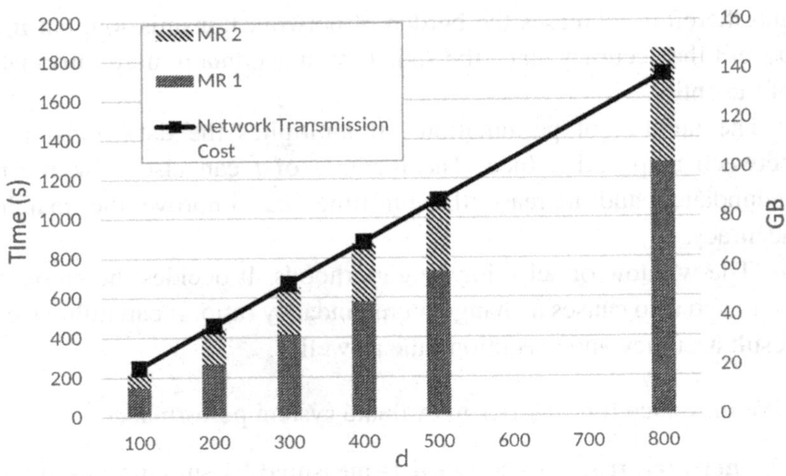

Fig. 3.11: Run-time and Network Transmission for Different Value of d ($t = 40$, $m = 8$)

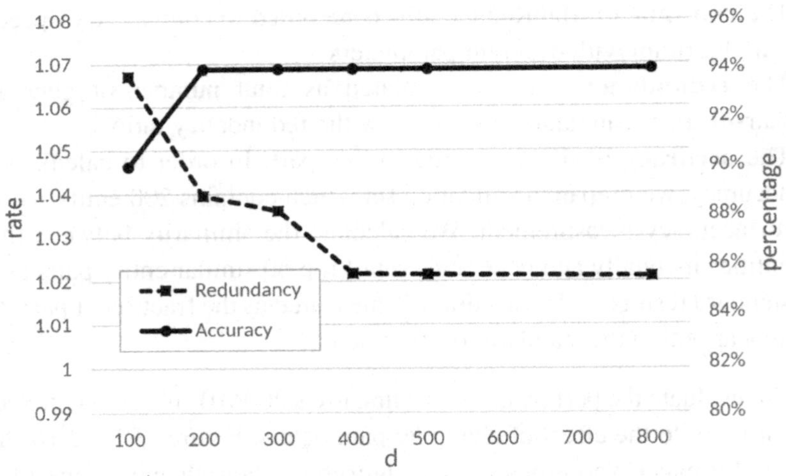

Fig. 3.12: Redundancy Rate and Accuracy for Different Value of d ($t = 40$, $m = 8$)

reason is that as the signature extends the differences between entities can be found more easily. So they may have fewer chances to be paired. Therefore, the redundancy rate decreases. The performance variations with changing t and m are listed in Figs. 3.13–3.16. Figures 3.13 and 3.15 shows similar performance with Fig. 3.11, but it seems that in Fig. 3.15, we spend large

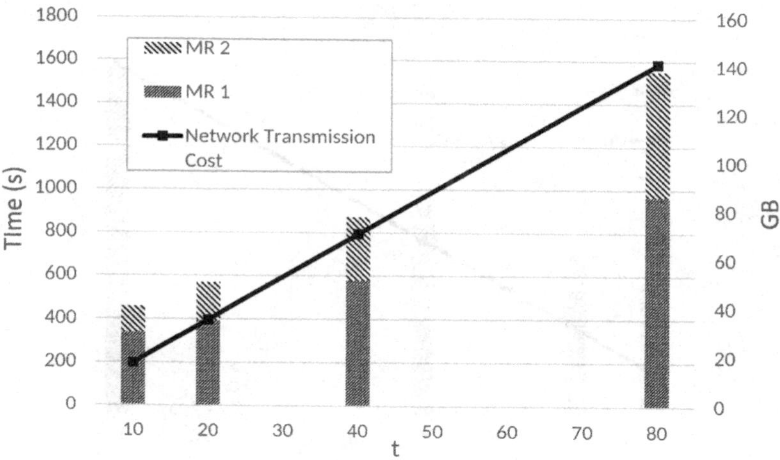

Fig. 3.13: Run-time and Network Transmission for Different Value of t ($d = 400$, $m = 8$)

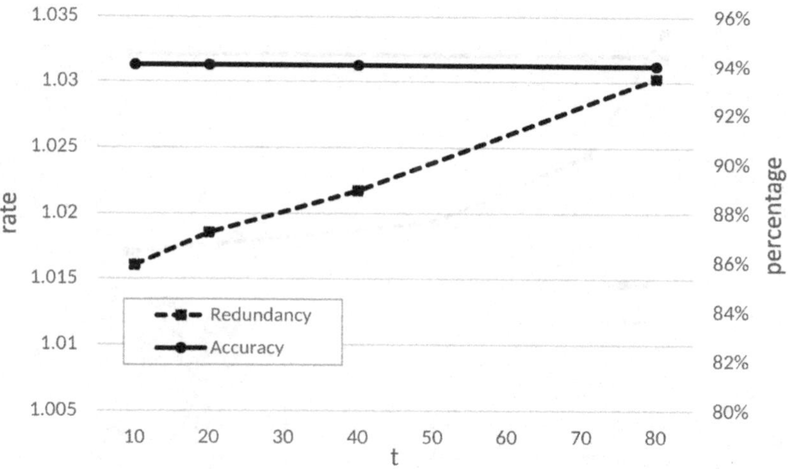

Fig. 3.14: Redundancy Rate and Accuracy for Different Value of t ($d = 400$, $m = 8$)

part of time on MR1 when $m = 2$ or $m = 4$. It is because a smaller m cannot reduce the cost on map phase when generating signatures and doing permutations. Figure 3.14 clearly shows that the number of permutations t can determine the redundancy rate directly.

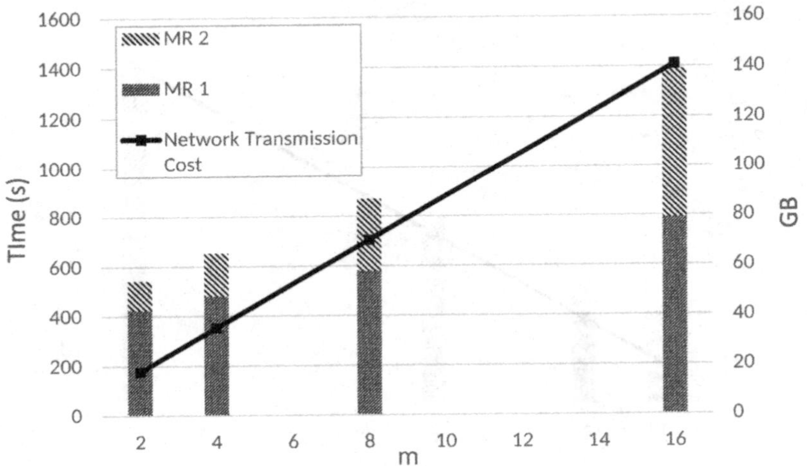

Fig. 3.15: Run-time and Network Transmission for Different Value of d ($t = 40$, $m = 8$)

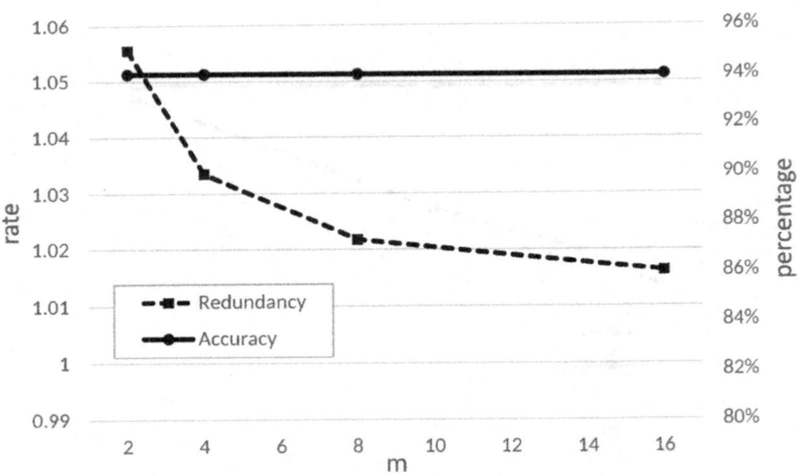

Fig. 3.16: Redundancy Rate and Accuracy for Different Value of m ($d = 400$, $t = 40$)

Generally speaking, all these three parameters can strongly influence the performance. Figures 3.11, 3.13 and 3.15 show that when $d \geq 400$, $t \leq 50$ and $m \geq 8$, we get a better performance on both redundancy rate and accuracy. So we choose $d = 500$, $t = 50$ and $m = 10$ to do the rest of the evaluations. Furthermore, the gradual growth of run-time when the dataset increases shows a good scalability of our matching method, which gives a huge advantage in processing big dataset. We also notice that the redundancy rate keeps fluctuating in a pretty low level, so it is not always necessary to add the deduplication MapReduce job.

Baseline Comparison. Our matching method aims at dramatically improving matching speed with a little sacrifice on matching accuracy. Hence, the *accuracy* and *run-time* metrics are suitable for evaluating our matching algorithm. The baseline methods are DSSJ and Dedoop.

In order to measure the accuracy, we use the validation set mentioned previously, and compare our matching result with DSSJ and Dedoop results. The standard result tests contain top 10, 20 and 50. Table 3.4 shows the accuracy of these top N tests. Since Dedoop compares all possible pairs of entities and calculates cosine similarity directly, the similarity result of Dedoop are always correct. However, the transmission cost is problematic that will be analyzed in the following content. When using the parameters ($d = 500$, $t = 50$, $m = 10$), we can get almost the same accuracy as DSSJ method does. At the same time, we evaluate the processing speed of our method comparing with Dedoop and DSSJ using these parameters. Figure 3.17 shows run-time between our method and the baseline methods. We just run a small size of data since the run-time of both Dedoop and DSSJ would exceed hours if the size of data is larger than 100 MB. The reason is that both of these two methods generate enormous size of pair candidates. We get nearly 100 GB map output data when running Dedoop on 200 MB dataset. It can burden the system drastically on network transmission and is hard to be processed in memory. On the contrary, our random-based matching method shows a good scalability on dataset size. The speed of

Table 3.4: Comparison of Accuracy Rate with DSSJ ($d = 500$, $t = 50$, $m = 10$)

Name	Top 10 (%)	Top 20 (%)	Top 50 (%)
DSSJ	90	95	94
Random-base Matching	90	100	94
Dedoop	100	100	100

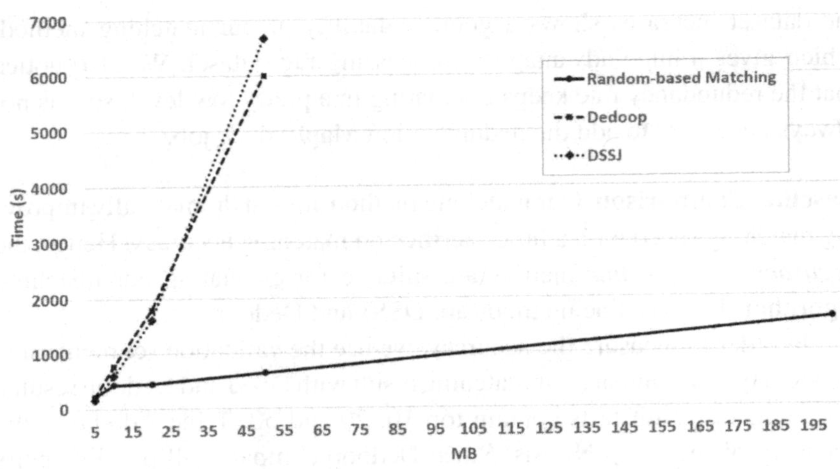

Fig. 3.17: Comparison of Run-time with Dedoop and DSSJ ($d = 500, t = 50, m = 10$)

our algorithm is significantly faster than Dedoop, and far more stable even when dealing with gigabytes of input data.

3.5 Conclusion

In this chapter, we design two entity resolution frameworks for different scenarios. One is a general learning-based framework including data preprocessing, i.e., schema integration and data cleaning, which reinforce each other, and another is an entity resolution that employs logistic regression model. This framework aims at improving the accuracy of entity resolution. It is implemented on centralized system and requires structured data as the input. As web data proliferate recently, another random-based framework is designed on distributed system, which consists of entity similarity calculation, candidate entity pair generation and implementation on MapReduce. It involves several random algorithms to boost the processing speed of entity resolution on semi-structured and unstructured entities.

Chapter 4

Review Selection

Online product reviews provide helpful information for user decision-making. However, since user-generated reviews have proliferated in recent years, it is critical to deal with the information overload in E-commerce sites. In this section, we propose an approach to select a small set of representative reviews for each product, which shall consider both attribute coverage and opinion diversity under the requirement of providing high quality reviews. We assign a weight to each attribute, which measures the attribute importance and helps to provide useful and important review set. Reviews are clustered into different groups representing different concerns which lead to better diversification results especially for selecting smaller sets of reviews.

4.1 Problem Definition

In this section, we give a formal definition to review selection problem and declare the properties of our problem.

Given an item $i \in I$, where I denotes a set of items in a certain product category, let $R = \{r_1, r_2, \ldots, r_n\}$ be a set of reviews commenting on i which cover a set of attributes $A = \{a_1, a_2, \ldots, a_m\}$ and express a set of opinions $O = \{o_1, o_2, \ldots, o_z\}$. We assume that reviewers may express two types of opinions on each attribute: positive or negative opinion. Hence, the size of O is $z = 2m$. A review r may cover a subset of attributes $A_r \subseteq A$ and express a subset of opinions $O_r \subseteq O$ on its attribute set.

Our task is to select a small set of reviews that have high quality, while at the same time covers important attributes with different opinions. We formalize our problem as shown in Problem 4.1.

Problem 4.1 (Diversified Review Selection). *Given a set of reviews R of an item i that covers a set of attributes A and expresses a set of opinions O, find a subset of reviews $S \subseteq R$ of size $|S| \leq k$ that maximize the overall value $F(S)$ of S :*

$$F(S) = (1 - \lambda)Q(S) + \lambda D(S), \tag{4.1}$$

where $Q(S)$ measures the quality of S, $D(S)$ rewards the diversity of S, k is an integer number and $\lambda \in [0, 1]$ is a diversity factor. The definition of $Q(S)$ and $D(S)$ is given in Section 4.2.

4.2 Quality and Diversity of Review Set

4.2.1 *The Quality of Review Set*

Since the overall quality of a review set is impacted by the quality of every single review in the set, we regard the quality of a review set as the average quality of reviews in the set. Therefore, the review set quality function $Q(S)$ is defined as follows:

$$Q(S) = \frac{\sum_{r \in S} q(r)}{|S|}, \tag{4.2}$$

where $q(r) \in [0, 1]$ measures the quality of review r.

Assessment of Review Quality. Motivated by the helpfulness vote mechanism adopted in E-commerce sites, we view the quality of a review as its proportion of helpfulness votes. Therefore, the review quality function $q(r)$ is defined as follows:

$$q(r) = \frac{q^{+}(r)}{q^{+}(r) + q^{-}(r)}, \tag{4.3}$$

where $q^{+}(r)$ (or $q^{-}(r)$) represents the number of users that consider review r helpful (or helpless).

However, some reviews such as newly-written reviews have few votes, which cannot properly estimate the quality of reviews, so instead of computing $q(r)$ directly, we use SVM regression to learn the function $q(r)$. It takes the following two steps to finish the task.

Step 1: It defines features impacting review quality. We consider two types of features: textual features [Kim *et al.* (2006)] and user preference features [Hong *et al.* (2012)], as shown in [Hong *et al.* (2012)], the combination of the two feature classes can improve the assessment. The textual features include the length and unigrams of a review, while the user preference features include the coverage of important attributes and the divergence from the mainstream viewpoint of a review. User preference features are defined below.

- **Attribute Coverage:** Covering as many attributes as possible is not enough, users pay more attention to those key attributes, so we consider the coverage of important attributes. Let $A_r \subseteq A$ be a set of attributes covered in review r, the coverage of important attributes $cov(r)$ is defined as follows:

$$cov(r) = \frac{\sum_{a \in A_r} w(a)}{\sum_{a' \in A} w(a')}, \tag{4.4}$$

  where $w(a) \in (0, 1)$ represents the weight of attribute a. We will introduce the attribute weight later.
- **Mainstream Divergence:** Users tend to consider helpful the reviews that follow the mainstream, so we measure the gap between the viewpoint of a review and the mainstream viewpoint. In E-commerce sites, users are required to give an item an overall rating ranging from one to five along with their reviews, so we can say that the overall rating expresses the same viewpoint as the review, and the average rating reflects the mainstream viewpoint. Therefore, the divergence from mainstream viewpoint $div(r)$ is defined as follows:

$$div(r) = \frac{\left| v(r) - \frac{\sum_{r' \in R} v(r')}{|R|} \right|}{max_{r' \in R} v(r')}, \tag{4.5}$$

  where $v(r) \in \{1, 2, \ldots, 5\}$ is the viewpoint of review r, $\frac{\sum_{r' \in R} v(r')}{|R|}$ is the mainstream viewpoint and $max_{r' \in R} v(r')$ is the maximum rating for normalization.

Step 2: It constructs training data for SVM regression. We randomly choose reviews with a certain amount of votes and estimate their quality according to $q(r)$ so as to form a labeled dataset of $(r, q(r))$ pairs. We employ the labeled dataset to train our regression model and use the model to estimate review quality.

Assignment of Attribute Weight. Users read reviews to get information about product attributes. However, the review collection of an item may cover dozens of attributes, while users are only interested in a part of important ones. In order to provide key information to users, we measure the importance of attributes and assign relevant weights.

According to user behaviors of review-writing, we regard attributes that are frequently referred in the reviews of an item and items in the same category as important attributes. Here, attributes that appear in the reviews of most items in a category are taken into consideration since they are common attributes for a category. When users are selecting items of this category, they are more likely to refer to those attributes first. Therefore, let $R_a \subseteq R$ be a set of review comments on an item $i \in I$ that cover attribute a, where I denotes a set of items in a certain category, and $I_a \subseteq I$ be a set of items that have reviews covering a, the attribute weight $w(a)$ is defined as follows:

$$w(a) = \frac{|R_a|}{max_{a' \in A}|R_{a'}|} \cdot \frac{|I_a|}{max_{a' \in A}|I_{a'}|}, \tag{4.6}$$

where $\frac{|R_a|}{max_{a' \in A}|R_{a'}|}$ measures the importance of a for an item and $\frac{|I_a|}{max_{a' \in A}|I_{a'}|}$ measures the importance of a for a category.

The definition of $w(a)$ is similar to that of TF–IDF, as an attribute can be viewed as a term, and the review collection of an item as a document. Hence, the importance of an attribute for an item is equal to TF, while the importance of an attribute for a category is equal to DF instead of IDF since we value attributes that are frequently referred in the reviews of items in the same category.

4.2.2 *The Diversity of Review Set*

Since each time we select one review to add into the review set, we regard the diversity of a review set as the sum of the diversity of each review in the set when it is selected. Therefore, the review set diversity function $D(S)$ is defined as follows:

$$D(S) = \sum_{r \in S} d(r), \tag{4.7}$$

where $d(r)$ evaluates the diversity of review r.

Diversification of Opinions. To diversify opinions in a review set, we take the following three-step method.

Step 1: We cluster reviews with similar concerns. We assume that there are l clusters, and randomly select l reviews to initialize each cluster. Since there may exist opinion sparsity in the review collection, we represent a review as a vector of TF–IDFs for the unigrams in the review. We compute the cosine distance between two review vectors as the similarity between them. Each time a review is added into a cluster based on the similarity between the review vector the cluster centroid vector, the cluster centroid vector will be updated accordingly.

Step 2: We decide the number of reviews selected from each cluster. We compute the proportion of each cluster in the review collection as the proportion of reviews from different clusters in the selected review set. Therefore, the proportion of reviews from cluster C_i in the selected review set is defined as follows:

$$p\left(C_i\right) = \frac{|C_i|}{|R|}. \tag{4.8}$$

Given an integer k as the size of the selected review set, the number of reviews selected from each cluster is defined as follows:

$$n\left(C_i\right) = \lfloor k \cdot p\left(C_i\right) + 1/2 \rfloor. \tag{4.9}$$

Step 3: We use MMR [Carbonell and Goldstein (1998)] to select reviews from different clusters. That is, in addition to the assumption that review r has not been added into S, it is in cluster C_i, and the number of reviews selected from C_i is less than $n\left(C_i\right)$, select r if it is similar with C_i, while at the same time not similar with S. Therefore, the review diversity function $d(r)$ is defined as follows:

$$d(r) = \lambda' sim\left(r, C_i\right) - \left(1 - \lambda'\right) sim(r, S), \tag{4.10}$$

where $\lambda' \in [0, 1]$ is a trade-off coefficient.

Here, let $O_r \subseteq O$ (or $O_{R'} \subseteq O$) be the set of opinions expressed by review r (or review set R'), the review similarity $sim\left(r, R'\right)$ is defined as follows:

$$sim\left(r, R'\right) = \frac{\sum_{o \in O_r \cap O_{R'}} w\left(a_o\right)}{\sum_{o' \in O_{R'}} w\left(a_{o'}\right)}, \tag{4.11}$$

where a_o represents the attribute corresponding to opinion o.

4.3 Review Selection Algorithm

In this section, we give algorithms to our problem including the algorithms for opinion extraction and review selection. Before we select reviews, we apply opinion extraction algorithm that extracts attributes and opinions from the original review collection to generate input for review selection algorithm.

4.3.1 *Opinion Extraction*

There are a number of researches [Hu and Liu (2004); Ding *et al.* (2008); Lu *et al.* (2009)] on extracting attributes and mining opinions from reviews. Our method is lexicon-based as well as rule-based to handle context-dependent opinion words. Given a review, it takes the following three steps.

First, extract opinion phrases. We define an opinion phrase (a, o) as a pair of attribute a and opinion word o. We refer to the approach proposed by Moghaddam and Ester (2012). They employ the grammatical relations produced by Stanford Dependency Parser [De Marneffe *et al.* (2006)] to define a set of dependency patterns, and generate opinion phrases according to the patterns.

Second, identify opinions expressed by opinion words in opinion phrases. There are two types of opinions: positive and negative opinion. Opinions are decided by opinion word lists [Hu and Liu (2004)], including a list of positive words and a list of negative words. If opinions cannot be determined according to the opinion word lists, we apply intra-sentence rule and inter-sentence rule [Ding *et al.* (2008)].

- **Intra-Sentence Rule:** Given an opinion word o and the sentence s where o is located in, identify its opinion by the other opinion words in s. This rule is based on the fact that if there are conjunctions such as "and" and "but" near o in s, we can decide its opinion by the opinion word o' on the other side of the conjunction.

- **Inter-Sentence Rule:** Given an opinion word o and the sentence s where o is located in, if s (or the next sentence to s) begins with a word like "but" or "however", it means o has different opinion from the opinion word in the last sentence (or the next sentence), otherwise they have the same opinion.

Finally, summarize opinions of attributes. Since an attribute may appear several times in a review, we aggregate all the opinions to produce an overall opinion. Given an attribute, if the number of positive opinions is larger than that of negative opinions, the attribute gains a positive opinion, or otherwise it gains a negative opinion.

4.3.2 *Review Selection*

We use a greedy algorithm to implement review selection as shown in Algorithm 4.1. The algorithm inputs a set of reviews $R = \{r_1, r_2, \ldots, r_n\}$, a set of attributes $A = \{a_1, a_2, \ldots, a_m\}$, a set of opinions $O = \{o_1, o_2, \ldots, o_z\}$ and an integer k, and outputs a subset of reviews $S \subseteq R$ of size $|S| \leq k$ as the result. It first clusters reviews according to their concerns (lines 1–10), and then selects reviews proportionally from different clusters to maximize the overall value of the selected review set (lines 11–16).

4.4 Experimental Results

In this section, we first introduce the dataset and parameter settings for experiments. Then, we measure the impact of diversity factor on the quality and diversity of the selected reviews. Finally, we compare our approach with the characteristic algorithms in aspects of review quality and diversity.

4.4.1 *Dataset and Settings*

In our experiments, we use data crawled from E-commerce site eBay.com. This dataset includes reviews from three categories: tablets and e-book readers, portable audio and digital cameras. There are 4,789 items and

Algorithm 4.1 Diversified Review Selection Algorithm

Input: a set of reviews $R = \{r_1, r_2, \ldots, r_n\}$; a set of attributes $A = \{a_1, a_2, \ldots, a_m\}$; a set of opinions $O = \{o_1, o_2, \ldots, o_z\}$; an integer k

Output: a subset of reviews $S \subseteq R$ of size $|S| \leq k$

randomly select $\{r_1, r_2, \ldots, r_l\} \subseteq R$
for $i = 1, \ldots, l$ **do**
  $C_i = \{r_i\}$
end for
for all $r \in R \setminus \{r_1, r_2, \ldots, r_l\}$ **do**
  cluster r
end for
for $i = 1, \ldots, l$ **do**
  compute $p(C_i), n(C_i)$
end for
$S = \emptyset$
for $i = 1, \ldots, k$ **do**
  $r = argmax_{r \in R \setminus S, r \in C_j, n(C_j) > 0} F(S \cup \{r\})$
  $S = S \cup \{r\}$
  $n(C_j) = n(C_j) - 1$
end for
return S

110,480 reviews in all. After pruning items having less than 20 reviews, there are 121 items on tablets and e-book readers with 9,555 reviews, 286 items on portable audio with 38,799 reviews and 583 items on digital cameras with 42,783 reviews. We find that only 21,101 reviews (i.e., 23.15%) from the total 91,137 reviews have helpfulness votes. Figure 4.1 shows the distribution of review numbers on different helpfulness vote numbers, from which the majority of reviews host few votes. Therefore, directly employing the proportion of helpfulness votes cannot accurately predict the quality of reviews.

In assessment of review quality, we select reviews having at least five votes as labeled data and use LIBSVM [Chang and Lin (2011)] to train our regression model. To measure our algorithm for quality assessment,

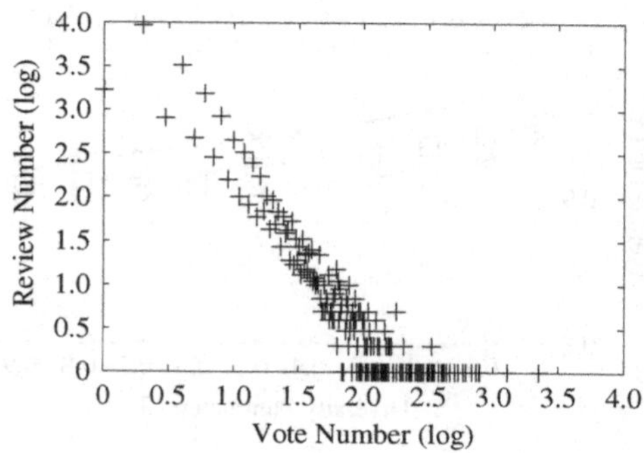

Fig. 4.1: Log–log Plot of Review Numbers on Vote Numbers

we select 60% of the labeled data as training data and the rest as test data to predict review quality. We adopt Pearson correlation coefficient as the metric to the correlation between the estimated quality and the labeled quality, so as to find whether the quality function is well learned. According to the evaluation by Kim *et al.* (2006), the resulting coefficient is around 0.5, so we set 0.5 as the borderline between well-learned quality functions and poorly-learned quality functions. Our algorithm results in a coefficient of 0.6405749, which is a little higher than 0.5. In diversification of opinions, since the size of the selected review set is small, we set the number of clusters as 3 to ensure the selection of reviews from each cluster. We set the trade-off coefficient λ' as 0.7.

4.4.2 *Evaluation on Diversity Factor*

In this section, we evaluate our algorithm for review selection. We set the size of the selected reviews as 5, 10 and 15, respectively. We apply the diversity factor with $\lambda \in \{0, 0.1, \ldots, 0.9\}$ to observe the effects on the quality and diversity of the selected review set with the increase of λ.

We are interested in how quality behaves when raising diversity factor λ from 0.1 up to 0.9, we hypothesize that the quality will reduce with the increase of λ. On the other hand, we will focus on checking whether attributes and opinions are diversified by our algorithm. In addition, we will compare our algorithm with other algorithms for review selection in both the quality and the diversity of the selected review set.

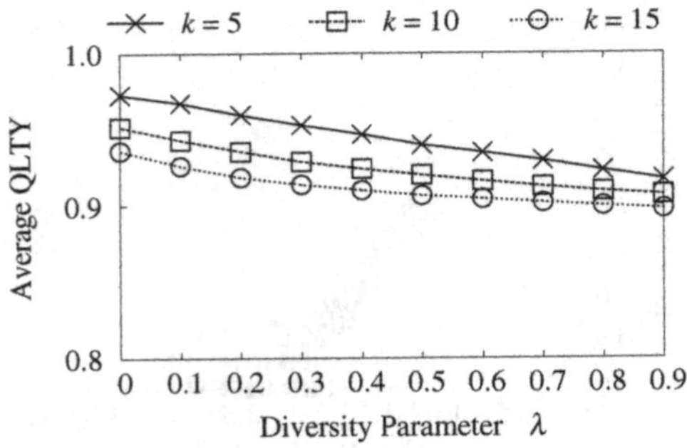

Fig. 4.2: Average Quality for Increasing λ

Review Set Quality Analysis. We apply our algorithm on all three categories of items and compute the average quality of all the selected review sets. As shown in Figure 4.2, the quality goes down smoothly when raising λ by 10% each time, which agrees with our hypothesis, and reveals that the diversification of review set has detrimental effects on the quality. This is because reviews with high quality may contain redundant attributes and similar opinions, so that they are not selected by our diversified algorithm.

Review Set Diversity Analysis. To decide whether attributes and opinions are diversified by our algorithm, we compute the average opinion coverage and the average cluster coverage of all the selected review sets. The opinion coverage includes opinion coverage and weighted opinion coverage. Let $O_S \subseteq O$ be the set of opinions expressed by the selected review set S,

- The **opinion coverage** is defined as:

$$cov_{\text{op}}(S) = \frac{|O_S|}{|O|}. \tag{4.12}$$

- The **weighted opinion coverage** is defined as:

$$cov_{\text{wop}}(S) = \frac{\sum_{o \in O_S \cap O} w(a_o)}{\sum_{o' \in O} w(a_{o'})}, \tag{4.13}$$

where a_o represents the attribute corresponding to opinion o.

The opinion coverage measures the diversity of opinions while the weighted opinion coverage measures the coverage of important attributes.

The cluster coverage includes cluster coverage and weighted cluster coverage, the definitions of which are similar with those of cov_{op} and cov_{wop}, except that O in the denominator is replaced by $O_{C_i} \subseteq O$. O_{C_i} is the set of opinions expressed by cluster C_i. After computing the cluster coverage for each cluster, we use the average cluster coverage as the result.

As depicted in Figs. 4.3 and 4.4, when $k = 5$ or 10 or 15 reviews are selected to generate the result set, the opinion coverage grows rapidly at first, peaking at approximately 31% or 45% or 56%, respectively, when $\lambda = 0.3$. However, the weighted opinion rises up to around 70% or 80% or

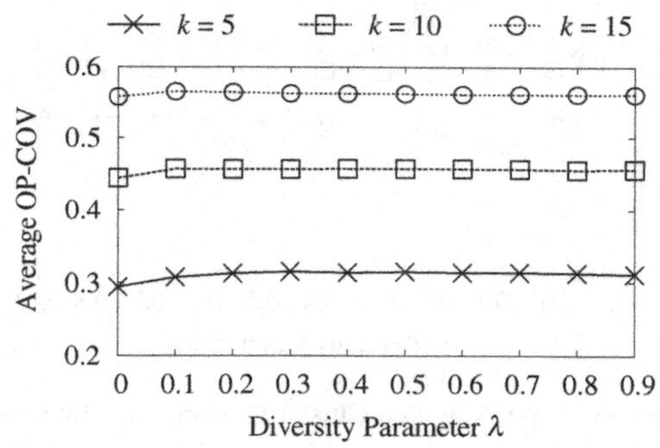

Fig. 4.3: Average Opinion Coverage for Increasing λ

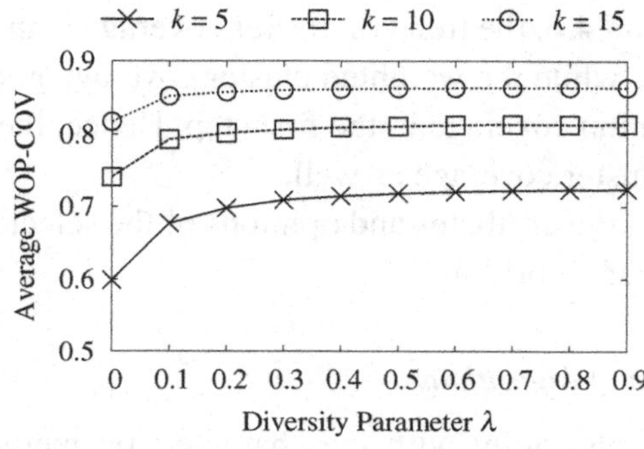

Fig. 4.4: Average Weighted Opinion Coverage for Increasing λ

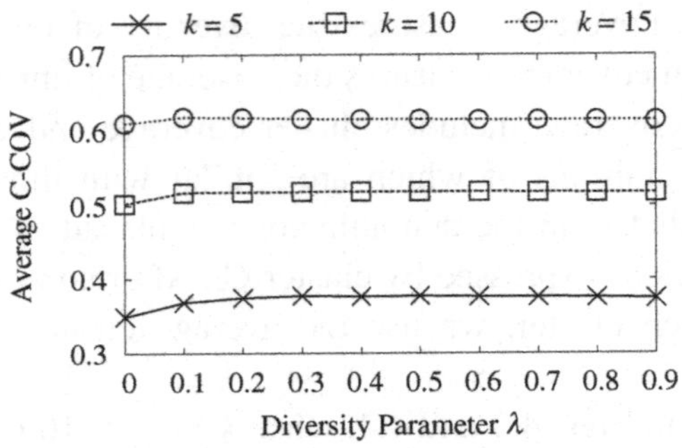

Fig. 4.5: Average Cluster Coverage for Increasing λ

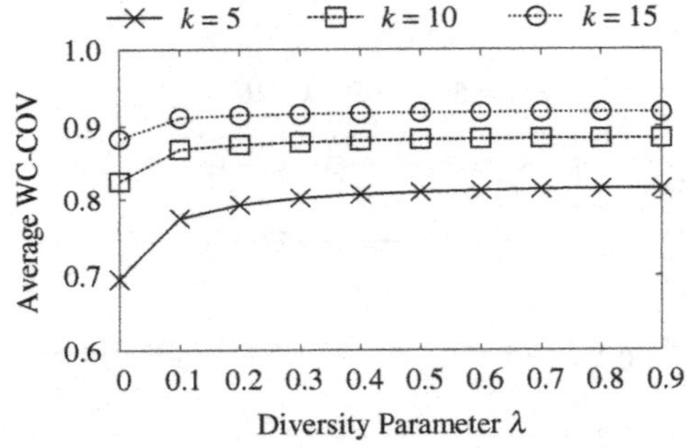

Fig. 4.6: Average Weighted Cluster Coverage for Increasing λ

85% and remains so afterwards. Hence, with the introduction of diversity factor λ, the opinion coverage improves.

In Figs. 4.5 and 4.6, the trend of cluster coverage is in line with that of opinion coverage, while the weighted cluster coverage goes up faster than the weighted opinion coverage in the first step. Hence, the diversity factor λ enhances the cluster coverage as well.

In conclusion, the attributes and opinions of the selected review set are diversified with our algorithm.

4.4.3 *Comparison of Algorithms*

We compare our algorithm with the characteristic method proposed by Lappas *et al.* (2012) that selects a set of reviews to promise the proportion of opinions in the review collection for an item. We implement the characteristic method with a greedy algorithm.

As presented in Review Set Diversity Analysis, the diversity of the selected review set reaches its peak when λ is 0.3, so we set λ as 0.3, and compare the average quality **QLTY**, the average (weighted) opinion coverage **(W)OP-COV** and the average (weighted) cluster coverage **(W)C-COV** of all the selected review sets produced by these two algorithms. We will also consider the average error of the proportion of opinions **PROP-ERR** as defined by Lappas *et al.* (2012).

In Table 4.1, our algorithm outperforms the characteristic algorithm in all aspects except **PROP-ERR**, when selecting $k = 5$, 10 and 15 reviews, respectively. Since the characteristic algorithm aims at reflecting the distribution of opinions in the review collection of an item, it is expected to perform better than our algorithm in **PROP-ERR**. However, since the size of the selected review set is small and the characteristic algorithm diversifies the selected review set by maintaining the proportion of opinions in the original review collection, some rarely mentioned attributes may not be covered. It may result in low coverage to some opinions with important attributes.

In our work, we define important attributes as those attributes that are frequently referred in the reviews of an item and items in the same category. Some attributes may only appear in a small fraction of reviews of an item, but they are likely to be important for the category where the item belongs to. For example, the reviews selected by our algorithm for **Canon EOS 1D 4.2 MP Digital SLR Camera** cover not only those common attributes

Table 4.1: Comparison between Characteristic Algorithm (CA) and Diversified Algorithm (DA)

k	Algorithm	QLTY	OP-COV	WOP-COV	C-COV	WC-COV	PROP-ERR
5	CA	0.8613	0.1008	0.4673	0.1705	0.6063	0.2177
	DA	0.9527	0.3148	0.7088	0.3771	0.8018	1.3087
10	CA	0.8615	0.2922	0.6780	0.3698	0.7922	0.1180
	DA	0.9287	0.4573	0.8059	0.5180	0.8786	0.5959
15	CA	0.8644	0.4725	0.7968	0.5380	0.8768	0.0668
	DA	0.9137	0.5617	0.8599	0.6151	0.9159	0.3632

such as:

- **picture quality**: "...It delivers excellent image quality, with great colors and detail..."
- **shooting**: "...I also like the 6.5fps shooting, which is handy for my wildlife shooting..."
- **price**: "...This is one of the best cameras out there for the price in my opinion..."

but also attributes that are not frequently mentioned in the reviews of this item while in fact are of great importance to the category of cameras, such as:

- **screen and interface**: "...What I love in it? Large viewfinder, great ISOs range, nice speed, large screen and comfortable interface..."
- **menu system**: "...The menu system is also very intuitive and easy to learn and the my menu feature is good for me about 90% of the time and keeps me from having to go through the whole menu interface..."

Users may concern about screen, interface and menu system when selecting cameras as they are key to user experience. Though they are not frequently referred in the reviews of this item, they are definitely important for the category of cameras.

4.5 Conclusion

We have proposed an approach to select a small set of reviews from the review collection of an item that have high quality, while at the same time have diversified attributes and opinions. We first train a regression model to estimate review quality. Then, we assign weights to attributes according to their importance, and to cover different opinions, we cluster reviews according to their opinion distributions and select reviews proportionally from different clusters. Finally, we use a diversity factor to balance the quality and diversity of the selected review set, and implement our method with a greedy algorithm to maximize the overall value of the selected review set.

Chapter 5

Review Summarization

This chapter presents two novel approaches to generate review summaries including scores and descriptive snippets for each product mentioned in a review. In one approach, we first extract context, i.e., snippets, that contains description of products from the huge comments, and choose snippets that express consumers' opinions on products. Secondly, we propose several methods to predict the ratings (from 1 to 5 stars) of evaluative snippets. Finally, we design two new snippet selection algorithms based on the standard seat allocation algorithm. They guarantee that the returned results preserve opinion-aspect statistical properties and attribute-aspect coverage. The core technique of the other approach is a new bilateral topic analysis model on the commentary text data. In the new model, the attributes discussed in the comments on dishes and users' evaluation on attributes are considered as two independent dimensions in the latent space. Combined with new opinionated word extraction and clustering-based representation selection algorithms, our new analysis technique is effective to generate high-quality summaries using representative snippets from the textual comments.

5.1 Problem Definition

As we propose two approaches to generate dish-level summaries in this chapter, which are diversity-based and topic model-based respectively, we formalize these two corresponding problems in this section.

5.1.1 *Diversify-based Summary Generation*

Given a set of reviews for a specific restaurant, our task is to generate a concise summary for each dish mentioned. The summary includes a score and the top K representative snippets for a dish. The notation of representative is defined with respect to the attributes and opinions of dishes. Hence, the quality of summary is measured by how well it covers the attribute-aspects and opinion-aspects of a dish.

We denote the collection of online reviews by $R = \{r\}$, where each $r \in R$ is associated with an overall score of s_r and a comment c_r. c_r may describe the opinions to several dishes $P_r = \{p\}$. Note that many restaurants may have dishes with the same name and we treat them as different dishes.

Definition 5.1 (Overall Score). An overall score s_r of a comment r is a numerical rating indicating different levels of the overall opinion, and $s_r \in [s_{min}, s_{max}]$. Usually, the range of s_r is from 1 (lowest) to 5 (highest), that is, $s_{min} = 1$ and $s_{max} = 5$.

Definition 5.2 (Product Snippet). A product snippet is extracted from review comments. The snippet sn_p is the descriptive context of a product p, which describes the user opinion on p but without a score.

Definition 5.3 (Product Modifier). Product modifiers $M = \{m\}$ are extracted from the product snippets. M_{sn} refers to the evaluative words or strings of sn. The modifiers are used for rating prediction of products.

Definition 5.4 (Snippet Score). A snippet score s_{sn} is the score of product snippet sn, showing the degree of satisfaction assigned by a user with the sentence in a comment. $s_{sn} \in [s_{min}, s_{max}]$.

Definition 5.5 (Dish Summary). A Dish summary PS_p is a set of dish snippets and a score s_p for a dish p. We have two sets of aspects, opinion-aspects, OT, and attribute-aspects, AT. Let $T = \{t_i\}$, where $t_i \in OT$ or $t_i \in AT$ indicates the set of aspects for a dish p and SN_p denotes a large set of snippets related to p. Let v_i indicate the popularity of the aspect t_i, which is the percentage of snippets in SN_p related to t_i. So PS_p is a diversity representation of SN_p with respect to T if and only if the number of snippets in SN_p is proportional to p_i for t_i.

5.1.2 *Topic Model-based Summary Generation*

Given the review comments from users on the dishes of the restaurants, we decompose the comments into snippets, such that each snippet is associated with a unique dish. Every snippet is thus modeled as a tuple $e = (r_i, d_j, w)$, in which r_i is the id of the restaurant, d_j is the id of the dish served by the restaurant r_i and w is a sequence of words $w = w_1 \dots w_l$ of length l describing the experience on dish d_j. A complete comment usually consists of a group of snippets discussing different dishes from a restaurant, and is associated with an overall evaluation score y as an integer between y_{min} and y_{max}. Typically, the range of score y is between $y_{min} = 1$ and $y_{max} = 5$ on real-world restaurant review sites.

The expected output of summarization based on text review comments includes a group of dishes from a particular restaurant, each of which contains score and representative text snippets with descriptions on the dish. In this chapter, we formulate the summarization as follows.

Problem 5.1 (Dish Summarization Problem). *For each dish d_j from restaurant r_i, given the snippet archive $E_{ij} = \{e_1, e_2, \dots, e_n\}$ on d_j and a specified positive integer k, the problem of dish summarization is to report a score $\hat{y}$ and extract k representative snippets, denoted by $\hat{E}_{ij}$.*

To quantitatively measure the goodness of summarization, we further define the representation closeness on the snippets, based on a certain distance measure over the domain of text snippets.

Definition 5.6 (Representation Closeness). Given a distance measure $D(\cdot, \cdot)$ defined over snippet pairs, the closeness of the summarization $\hat{E}_{ij}$, with respect to the text archive E_{ij}, is defined as

$$D(\hat{E}_{ij}, E_{ij}) = \sum_{e \in E_{ij}} \min_{\hat{e} \in \hat{E}_{ij}} D(\hat{e}, e).$$

Intuitively, the closeness measure tells how representative the selected snippets are when compared against the whole archive of snippets regarding the specific dish. It is thus straightforward to implement the dish summarization by minimizing the representation closeness when selecting the representative text snippets.

5.2 Diversity-based Approach

We propose a three-step approach to perform the dish summarization task defined in Section 5.1.1: (1) find the evaluative snippets; (2) predict the snippet scores; (3) summarize the dish-related snippets.

5.2.1 *Finding Evaluative Snippets*

In this step, our target is to obtain evaluative snippets from the comments. First, we identify the dishes in each restaurant. Then, we extract the context around the dish as dish snippets. Finally, we classify the snippets.

To identify dishes, we simply suppose that we have a list of dishes for each restaurant. Then, we identify the dishes in the comments based on the list. To extract snippets, however, the texts in online reviews are often informal. That is, in many cases there are no clear boundaries for sentences. Thus, if we cannot identify a formal sentence, we set a window to extract the word strings that include left and right N ($N = 10$ in our experiments) words surrounding the dish.

For our task, we need opinionated snippets to describe product quality. However, not all the snippets we extract are helpful for users to judge dish quality. For example, in a Chinese restaurant, a snippet "I ordered the Chicken Rice" is not opinionated because it just says that the user ate the Chicken Rice, but does not have any information about the quality. However, "The Chicken Rice is delicious and the chicken is tender" and "Chicken Rice is not good" are expressive opinions because they praise or depreciate the food.

Clearly, identifying the opinionated snippets is a classification problem with two classes, opinionated and non-opinionated. The classification problem is typically solved by supervised classifiers, such as Naïve Bayes [McCallum *et al.* (1998)], Maximum Entropy (ME) [Berger *et al.* (1996)] and Support Vector Machines (SVM) [Vapnik (1995)]. The supervised classifiers require labeled data for training. However, it is hard to scale and apply to a new domain due to the cost of manual labeling of training data.

Alternately, we propose a novel unsupervised method which only utilizes the comments and the overall scores available in online review sites. The method is based on the entropy in information theory. It contains the following steps: (1) extract product modifiers; (2) calculate the distribution of N-grams; (3) compute the entropy; (4) perform classification.

(1) Extract product modifiers. The product modifiers are not easy to extract. In previous works [Qiu *et al.* (2011); Zhai *et al.* (2011)], the existing techniques used dependency relations between the product and its modifiers or Part-of-Speech tags near to the products. However, the current dependency parsers and Part-of-Speech taggers do not perform well for informal texts [Petrov and McDonald (2012)]. Instead, we use N-gram word strings as the product modifiers. We filter out high frequency words using a stop word list. Thus, each snippet is represented as $sn = \{ng_1, \ldots, ng_i, \ldots, ng_n\}$, where ng_i refers to a N-gram word string (1-gram or 2-gram here).

(2) Calculate the distribution of N-grams. We calculate the distribution d_{ng} of ng over the overall scores (from s_{min} to s_{max}). The distribution is computed as follows:

$$d_{ng} = [p_{s_{min}}(ng), \ldots, p_{s_i}(ng), \ldots, p_{s_{max}}(ng)] \tag{5.1}$$

$$p_{s_i}(ng) = \frac{N(ng, s_i)}{\sum_j (N(ng, s_j))},$$

where $N(ng, s_i)$ refers to the average number of snippets containing N-gram string ng with the overall score $s_i \in [s_{min}, s_{max}]$.

(3) Compute the entropy. Based on the entropy in information theory, if a N-gram string is used in the snippets with a wide range of scores, especially with equal probability, the ambiguity of the string tends to increase. On the other hand, if the string centers on few specific scores, this tends to increase the specificity of the string. The entropy of a string ng is as follows:

$$E(ng) = \sum_i p_{s_i}(ng) \log(p_{s_i}(ng)).$$

Finally, we accumulate the entropy of N-gram strings in each snippet and obtain the average entropy of the snippet. The average entropy of snippet sn is:

$$AE_{sn} = \frac{\sum_i E(ng_i)}{n}. \tag{5.2}$$

(4) Perform classification. We rank the snippets in decreasing order of their average entropies and use a threshold to classify the snippets. The threshold value is tuned on the development set.

5.2.2 *Predicting Snippet Scores*

Now, we have the evaluative snippets for each dish. We want to predict the score for each snippet without any supervision nor any external knowledge. We propose several methods to predict the score and the score is of the same scale as the overall score.

Direct Prediction. In this method, we assume that the opinions to the dishes in the comments are consistent to the overall score a user gives. That is, each snippet included in a comment has the same score as the overall score of the comment. Here, we only use the direct information which is the overall score of the comment that the snippet is included in. The snippet score of direct prediction is:

$$s_{dir}(sn) = s(r),\ sn \in r. \tag{5.3}$$

Average Prediction. The first method is very simple. However, in real data, we often find that the users have different opinions on different dishes in one comment. For example, in "The Chicken Rice is delicious, and the chicken is tender. But the Duck Soup is not good", the consumer gives a positive opinion on "Chicken Rice" and a negative opinion on "Duck Soup". Thus instead, we use the average score of N-gram strings to predict the snippet score. The score of N-gram string is evaluated by using the information of the overall scores of all reviews. The score of ng is,

$$s(ng) = \frac{\sum_{r \in R_{ng}} s(r)}{|R_{ng}|}, \tag{5.4}$$

where R_{ng} is the set of reviews containing modifier ng, and $|R_{ng}|$ is the number of R_{ng}. Then the snippet score of average prediction is,

$$s_{ave}(sn) = \frac{\sum_{ng \in sn} s(ng)}{N_{sn}}, \tag{5.5}$$

where N_{sn} is the number of N-gram strings included in sn.

Max Prediction. In the second method, we use the average rating. Here, we use the maximum rating. The snippet score of *max* prediction is,

$$s_{max}(sn) = max_{ng} s(ng). \tag{5.6}$$

Score of Products. Based on the snippet scores, we calculate the average score for each product. The product score is,

$$s(p) = \frac{\sum s(sn_p)}{N_p}, \tag{5.7}$$

where N_p is the number of snippets p has.

5.2.3 *Summarizing Product Snippets*

In this step, we perform product summarization based on the candidate snippets of products provided in Section 5.2.1. Our target is to choose a set of snippets with approximate diversification which considers both the opinion-aspects and attribute-aspects. We first introduce a standard method for finding proportional representations used to solve the seat allocation problem. We then build the connection between this problem and our problem of diversification. Two novel algorithms are derived from the standard seat allocation algorithm for product summarization.

Seat Allocation. The standard seat allocation algorithm, named Sainte–Lagüe method, is introduced for document summarization by Dang and Croft (2012). We adapt it for item clusters. The new algorithm is shown in Algorithm 5.1. We consider all the available slots iteratively. In each iteration, we compute a quotient for all the clusters based on the members they have and the number of slots they have taken, see line 4, where v_i

---

Algorithm 5.1 The slot allocation for clusters

1: $s_i = 0, \forall i$
2: **for** all available slots **do**
3:     **for** all clusters P_i **do**
4:         $quot[i] = \frac{v_i}{2 \times s_i + 1}$
5:     **end for**
6:     $k = argmax_i quot[i]$
7:     m^* = one member of M_k
8:     Assign the current slot to m^*
9:     $M_k = M_k - \{m^*\}$
10:     $s_k = s_k + 1$
11: **end for**

---

is the number of members party P_i has, and s_i is the number of slots the party has taken. The current slot is assigned to the cluster with the largest quotient (line 6), which helps maintain the overall proportionality. The selected cluster chooses one of its members to the slot (lines 8 and 9, where M_k is the members of P_k). Finally, it increases the number of slots assigned to the selected cluster by one. The procedure continues until all the slots are occupied.

Flat Diversification. We first only consider the opinion-aspects which are generated based on the snippet scores predicted in Section 5.2.2. Let p indicate the product searched by the user, $OT = \{t_i\}$ indicate the opinion-aspects for p. $SN_p = \{sn_1, \ldots, sn_n\}$ is the candidate snippets with predicted scores given by Section 5.2.2. The task is to select subset $PS_p@K$ of SN_p to form a summary of size K for product p.

Our idea is to select a subset as the summary with higher opinion diversity. The optimal subset, consequently, is a set in which the number of snippets relevant to the opinion-aspect t_i is proportional to its popularity v_i. This objective is very similar to that of the seat allocation problem mentioned above. As a result, we derive a framework for opinion diversification directly from Algorithm 5.1.

We consider the situation where a snippet is relevant to only one aspect. That is, all the snippets are grouped into one of clusterings by a predefined criterion. The new algorithm is shown in Algorithm 5.2. We predefine K slots available for assignment. First, we compute the vote each aspect should receive based on SN_p (line 2). We have a cluster for each aspect and then the snippets are grouped into one of the clusters by considering the predicted scores. The number of snippets in each cluster is the vote. The function for mapping sn to cluster cl is,

$$cl(sn) = \begin{cases} t_1, \ \mathrm{s(sn)} \leq 1.5 \\ t_2, \ 1.5 < \mathrm{s(sn)} \leq 2.5 \\ t_3, \ 2.5 < \mathrm{s(sn)} \leq 3.5 \\ t_4, \ 3.5 < \mathrm{s(sn)} \leq 4.5 \\ t_5, \ 4.5 < \mathrm{s(sn)}. \end{cases}$$

In each iteration, we compute a quotient for all the aspects based on the votes they receive and the number of slots they have taken, see line 5,

Algorithm 5.2 Flat diversification

1: $s_i = 0, \forall i, SN_p$
2: compute v based on SN_p
3: **for** all available slots (predefined K) **do**
4:     **for** all opinion aspects $t_i \in OT$ **do**
5:         $quot[i] = \frac{v_i}{2 \times s_i + 1}$
6:     **end for**
7:     $k = argmax_i quot[i]$
8:     sn_p^* = find the best snippet with respect to t_k
9:     $SN_p = SN_p - sn_p^*$
10:     $PS_p@K = PS_p@K \bigcup \{s_p^*\}$
11:     $s_k = s_k + 1$
12: **end for**

where v_i is the number of votes aspect t_i receives, and s_i is the number of slots they have taken. The current slot is assigned to the aspect with the largest quotient (line 7). We choose the best snippet with respect to t_k to the slot (lines 9 and 10, where SN_p is the remaining snippets). Finally, it increases the number of slots assigned to the selected aspect by one. The procedure continues until all slots are occupied. $PS_p@K$ is the output of the algorithm.

Hierarchical Diversification. In the above method, we only consider the opinion-aspects. Here, we propose a hierarchical diversification method by considering both opinion-aspects and attribute-aspects. Because the two aspects describe the different views, it is hard to design a simple way similar to Algorithm 5.2. We design a method of the summarization, called hierarchical diversification, based on the hierarchical structure. We use clustering methods to build hierarchical trees for the candidate snippets. Based on the tree, we design a new algorithm for diversification.

One key step for snippet clustering is the representation of snippets. We represent a snippet as a vector that includes three factors: (1) modifiers that are N-gram strings; (2) snippet clusters $cl(sn)$ that are described in the above section; (3) word clusters. The factor of snippet clusters is related to the opinion-aspects. To bridge different words used by different users, which describe the same attribute, we employ word clustering to acquire the knowledge about paradigmatic lexical relations from all the comment texts. Our work is inspired by the successful application to syntactic parsing [Koo *et al.* (2008)]. Following their work, we also use the Brown word clustering algorithm that generates a hard clustering, each word belongs to exactly one cluster. We use the ids of snippet clusters and word clusters and N-gram strings in the vectors of snippets.

For snippet clustering, there are many clustering algorithms available for building the trees. Here, we use the tool "CLUTO".[1] In the hierarchical clustering solution, the objects of each cluster form a subtree, and the different subtrees are merged to get an all inclusive cluster at the end. The hierarchical agglomerative clustering is computed so that it optimizes the clustering criterion function named $I2$ (the details can be found in [Zhao and Karypis (2001)]). Figure 5.1 shows an example of hierarchical tree where the leaf nodes are the snippets (from 0 to 9).

The vote for each cluster is the number of snippets it includes. We treat the leaf node as a single cluster containing only one member. For example, cluster 18 has 10 votes, cluster 10 has 2 votes and cluster 9 has 1 vote in Fig. 5.1.

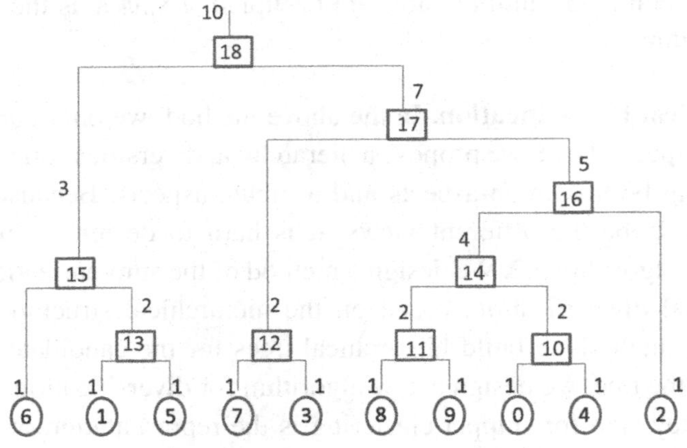

Fig. 5.1: An Example of Hierarchical Tree

[1] http://glaros.dtc.umn.edu/gkhome/views/cluto.

Algorithm 5.3 Hierarchical diversification

```
 1: s_i = 0, ∀i, SN_p
 2: compute v for each cluster in the tree
 3: for all available slots (predefined K) do
 4:     cid = ROOT
 5:     while cid is not a leaf node do
 6:         for each ch ∈ children of cid do
 7:             quot[ch] = v_ch / (2 × s_ch + 1)
 8:         end for
 9:         cid = argmax_ch quot[ch]
10:     end while
11:     sn_p^cid is the snippet in cluster cid
12:     SN_p = SN_p − sn_p^cid
13:     PS_p@K = PS_p@K ⋃ {sn_p^cid}
14:     update s for the clusters on the path from cid to ROOT
15: end for
```

We now provide a new algorithm for hierarchical diversification. The algorithm is shown in Algorithm 5.3. We first compute the votes for all the clusters in the tree in line 2. From line 4 to 10, we find the best snippet from the candidates through the tree. We go down from the ROOT and compare the quotients of the children of current cluster. At the end of this step, we obtain a cluster containing only one leaf node (sn_p^{cid}). sn_p^{cid} is selected to the slot (lines 12 and 13). Finally, we increase the number of slots assigned to the clusters on the path from *cid* to ROOT. The procedure continues until all the slots are occupied. We also obtain the $PS_p@K$ as the final output.

5.3 Topic Model-based Approach

For the problem defined in Section 5.1.2, we design a topic model-based framework to transform the original text comments with scores into dish summarization results as follows.

Pre-processing: The first phase applies natural language processing techniques to extract the snippets, i.e., short text subsequences from the original text review comments. There are three major missions in this step, including *identification* of dish names of the restaurant, *decomposition* of the texts into snippets of specified length and *binding* between dish names and snippets. We simply employ well-recognized algorithms in the literature, which is declared in Section 5.2.1.

Modeling: The second phase runs *Modeling* analysis on the the snippets, using graphical model techniques over the texts in the snippets and the scores on the comments. The goal of the text analysis on the snippets is to understand the latent topics and latent scores of the snippets extracted from the first pre-processing step. Then, different tags are attached to each of the result snippet. For example, one snippet is associated with a tag (taste, 5), indicating that this snippet expresses highly positive opinion on the taste. Such result tags are fed into the final summarization step for further processing in the framework.

Summarization: The third phase conducts the final *Summarization* for each dish of the restaurants. Given the tags on each snippet regarding a particular dish, the framework calculates an average score of the dish on all aspects discussed by the users. It also selects k representative snippets, based on the principle of representation closeness proposed in Section 5.1.2. Section 5.3.3 looks into the summarization problem from an algorithmic perspective.

5.3.1 *Bilateral Topic Model*

Our new generative model is motivated by the observations that word co-occurrences in the review comments reflect two different types of correlations, i.e., aspect correlation and score correlation, at the same time. It basically implies that two words frequently co-appearing in review comments indicate the correlation between these words in terms of certain aspect or certain score. Such bilateral correlation is not considered in any of the existing models, e.g., LDA and its variants, mainly due to the limited influence of numerical scores in specific text domains, e.g., news. To better capture the latent aspect and score in dish review comments, however, we have to incorporate such two types of correlations into a unified topic model, leading to the *Bilateral Topic Model* (BTM) proposed in this section.

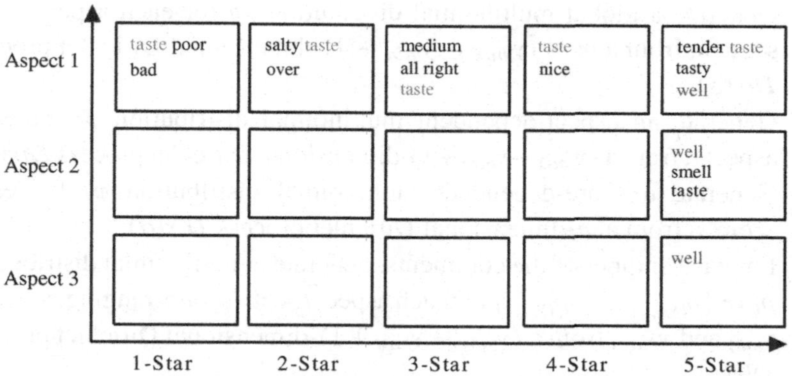

Fig. 5.2: An Example of Topic Matrix and Keywords with Topics

The basic assumption in the bilateral topic model is that the general topics of the review comments can be embedded into a 2-dimensional discrete space, with *aspect* and *score* as two independent dimensions. In Fig. 5.2, we present an example of the topic matrix, in which each cell denotes a topic associated with a pair of aspect and score on the dish, along with a group of relevant words used under the topic. The first row in the matrix, for example, covers topics related to the taste of the food, with "taste" as a common distinguishing keyword against topics on other rows. The right-most column in the matrix covers topics related to highest scores on all aspects, with "well" as a frequent word present in the corresponding snippets. Obviously, the bilateral model on the topics contains correlations on both dimensions, when such common keywords are shared by the topic cells on same row or same column.

Given such a bilateral topic matrix, we further assume that the restaurant review comments are generated by the stochastic process described below. Generally speaking, the users generate a topic distribution over the pairs of aspect and score, randomly select one pair of aspect and score for every word slot in the snippet, and pick up a word for the slot based on a dictionary corresponding to the aspect-score pair.

(1) Generate a global multinomial distribution for all comments, i.e., $\theta = (\theta_1, \theta_2, \ldots, \theta_m)$ on m aspects, from a Dirichlet process $Dir(\beta)$.

(2) Generate a global multinomial distributions ϕ for each aspect t and score s, from a $m \times (y_{max} - y_{min} + 1)$-dimensional Dirichlet process $Dir(\alpha)$.
(3) Generate an aspect-dependent multinomial distribution ϕ_t for each aspect t, from a $(y_{max} - y_{min} + 1)$-dimensional Dirichlet process $Dir(\alpha)$.
(4) Generate a score-dependent multinomial distribution ϕ_s for each score s, from a m-dimensional Dirichlet process $Dir(\alpha)$.
(5) For each snippet of the comments, generate a multinomial distribution $\rho_t = \{\rho_{ty_{min}}, \ldots, \rho_{ty_{max}}\}$ for each aspect t, with scores ranging between y_{min} and y_{max}, from a $(y_{max} - y_{min} + 1)$-dimensional Dirichlet process $Dir(\gamma)$.
(6) For each word in the snippet at position p, select a pair of aspect and score $z_p = (t, s)$ based on the probability $\{\rho_{ts}\}$.
(7) For each word in the snippet at position p, choose a distribution from $\{\phi, \phi_t, \phi_s\}$ based on constant probabilities $c = (c_0, c_1, c_2)$.
(8) Generating z_p based on $\{\rho_t\}$. Pick up a word w_p using the multinomial distribution chosen in the previous step.
(9) After generating all words for the snippet, randomly choose one z_p from all of its snippets to generate the overall score of the comment, i.e., y.

The generative model shown in Fig. 5.3 simulates a simplified but meaningful procedure for ordinary people's restaurant comment writing. In particular, the key difference between bilateral topic model and standard LDA is the selection of words for the snippets (steps 7 and 8 in the generative model above). There are three independent candidate multinomial distributions, ϕ on all aspect-score pairs, ϕ_t on aspects and ϕ_s on scores, respectively. The coin controlling probabilities (c_0, c_1, c_2), with $c_0 + c_1 + c_2 = 1$, are used to select one of the multinomial distributions. In Fig. 5.4, we present an example to elaborate the vocabulary selection and word pickup process, with inputs ϕ, ϕ_t, ϕ_s and c. Each solid square in the figure denotes a multinomial distribution on the vocabulary. After the generation of z_p = (taste, 5), the coin variable is flipped, under the example probabilities $c_0 = 0.4$, $c_1 = 0.3$ and $c_2 = 0.3$. If coin c selects ϕ, the generative model chooses the multinomial distribution based on both

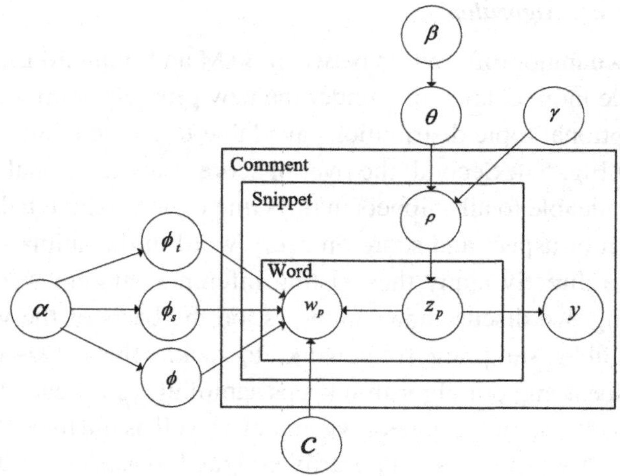

Fig. 5.3: Graphical Model of Generative Procedure

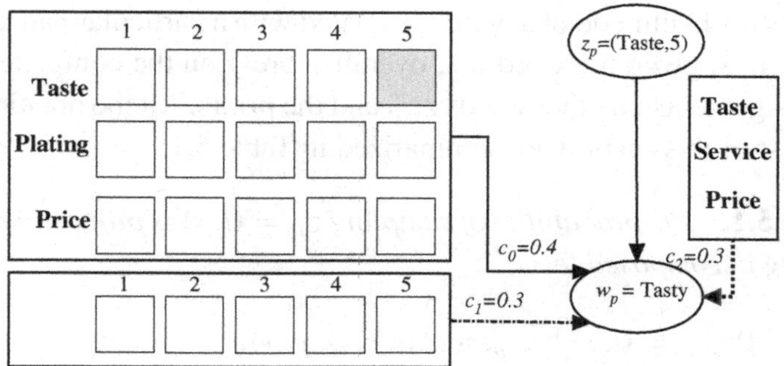

Fig. 5.4: An Example of Vocabulary Selection and Word Pickup in BTM

t and s in z_p. If c opts to return ϕ_t (ϕ_s resp.) otherwise, the model picks up a multinomial distribution based on t (s resp.) only. Finally, the model adds a word into the text, by choosing the word based on the returned multinomial distribution on the vocabulary. Such generative model naturally reflects correlation on aspects and correlation on scores, due to the possibility of adopting multinomial distributions with respect to ϕ_t and ϕ_s for certain number of words.

5.3.2 *Inference Algorithm*

There are two major differences between BTM and standard LDA, making the inference more challenging under the new problem setting. First, there are three optional topic distributions available to the generative model, as is shown in Fig. 5.4. Second, the overall score is an additional observable variable applicable to all snippets in the same review, which helps to guide the selection of aspect and score on every word in the snippets. It is thus nontrivial to directly apply the existing inference strategies for LDA. In the following, we discuss new strategies, on the basis of the well-known collapsed Gibbs sampling framework, to tackle these two difficulties. Generally speaking, our algorithm keeps sampling z_p for each word w_p in the snippets, based on the generative model as well as the hyperparameters. An instance of word w_p is temporarily assigned to aspect t and score s by the sampling algorithm, if $z_p = (t, s)$ after a sampling iteration. The key of our new algorithm is to run appropriate sampling on $z_p = (t, s)$ based on a valid probability close to $\Pr(z_p = (t, s) \mid z_{-p}, w_p, \alpha, c, \beta, \gamma, y)$, which estimates the likelihood of a word associated with a particular pair of aspect t and score s, given the word w_p, overall score y on the complete review, topic assignments on other words z_{-p} and the priors. All the notations used in the rest of this section are summarized in Table 5.1.

Lemma 5.1. *The probability of sampling $z_p = (t, s)$ is proportional to the following decomposed form,*

$$\begin{aligned} &\Pr(z_p = (t, s) \mid z_{-p}, w_p, \alpha, c, \beta, \gamma, y), \\ &\propto \Pr(z_p = (t, s) \mid z_{-p}, w_p, \alpha, c, \beta, \gamma) \cdot \Pr(y \mid z_p, z_{-p}). \end{aligned} \tag{5.8}$$

The proof of the lemma above is straightforward, based on the graphical model in Fig. 5.3, and thus skipped here.

Since there are three different generative schemes on w_p, $\Pr(z_p = (t, s) \mid z_{-p}, w_p, \alpha, c, \beta, \gamma)$ adopts different calculation equations in terms of the value of random coin c. When c chooses ϕ, the generation process degenerates to the standard LDA with $m \times (y_{max} - y_{min} + 1)$ topics. Similarly, when c chooses ϕ_t (resp. ϕ_s), it results in a LDA model with m topics (resp. $y_{max} - y_{min} + 1$ scores). This observation motivates us to estimate the conditional probability on $z_p = (t, s)$ by combining the

Table 5.1: Table of Notations in Section 5.3

Symbol	Description
W	the size of the word dictionary
t	an aspect of dish comments
α, β, γ	Dirichlet priors parameters in the generative model
w_p	a word at position p in the corresponding snippet
z_p	assignment of w_p to an aspect-score pair
z_{-p}	assignments of all words to aspect-score pairs except w_p
m	number of aspects
y_{min}, y_{max}	minimal and maximal scores
y, s	concrete scores between y_{min} and y_{max}.
c_0, c_1, c_2	switching probabilities on multinomial distributions
$N_{-p,ts}^{(w_p)}$	the sum on aspect t and score s over word w_p except the current occurrence
$N_{-p,ts}^{(\cdot)}$	the sum on aspect t and score s over all words except w_p
$N_{-p,t\cdot}^{(\cdot)}$	the sum on aspect t over all words except w_p
$N_{-p,\cdot s}^{(\cdot)}$	the sum on score s over all words except w_p
$N_{-p,\cdot\cdot}^{(\cdot)}$	the sum on all aspects and scores over all words except w_p
e_l	an extracted snippet from the comments
$\|e_l\|$	the number of words in the snippet e_l
S	total number of words in all snippets from an individual comment
Q	maximal number of iterations
L	total number of words in all snippets from all comments
d_j	the summarization target dish
$\hat{y}$	the estimated score on particular dish
E_{ij}	snippets with respect to a dish d_j from restaurant r_i
$\mathscr{S}(r_i, d_j, t)$	the score of d_j from restaurant r_i on aspect t
P_l	the distribution of snippet e_l on aspect-score domain

probabilities from three independent LDAs, formalized by the following lemma.

Lemma 5.2. *The first component of Equation (5.8), i.e., the probability* $\Pr(z_p = (t, s) \mid z_{-p}, w_p, \alpha, c, \beta, \gamma)$*, is estimated by:*

$$\Pr(z_p = (t, s) \mid z_{-p}, w_p, \alpha, c, \beta, \gamma)$$

$$= c_0 \frac{N_{-p,ts}^{(w_p)} + \beta\gamma}{N_{-p,ts}^{(\cdot)} + W\beta\gamma} \frac{N_{-p,ts}^{(\cdot)} + \alpha}{N_{-p,\cdot\cdot}^{(\cdot)} + m\,(y_{max} - y_{min})\,\alpha}$$

$$+c_1 \frac{N_{-p,ts}^{(w_p)} + \beta}{N_{-p,ts}^{(\cdot)} + W\beta} \frac{N_{-p,ts}^{(\cdot)} + \alpha}{N_{-p,\cdot s}^{(\cdot)} + m\alpha}$$

$$+c_2 \frac{N_{-p,ts}^{(w_p)} + \gamma}{N_{-p,ts}^{(\cdot)} + W\gamma} \frac{N_{-p,ts}^{(\cdot)} + \alpha}{N_{-p,t\cdot}^{(\cdot)} + (y_{max} - y_{min})\alpha}. \tag{5.9}$$

Basically, the equation above consists of three different estimations, using the independent topics, aspect-dependent topics and score-dependent topics. These estimations are aggregated using the weights c_0, c_1 and c_2.

Regarding the second component in Equation (5.8), i.e., the probability $\Pr(y \mid z_p, z_{-p})$, we can easily derive the following lemma for the probability evaluation, based on the given generative process of the overall score y. It generally aggregates overall words in the snippets and simulates the likelihood of selecting a particular score y, with $I(\cdot)$ as an indicator function returning 1 when the condition is satisfied, and returning 0 otherwise.

Lemma 5.3. *If there are n snippets associated with a particular review containing word w_p, i.e., $E = \{e_1, e_2, \ldots, e_n\}$, the second component of Equation 5.8, i.e., the probability $\Pr(y \mid z_p, z_{-p})$, could be estimated as:*

$$\Pr(y \mid z_p, z_{-p}) = \frac{\sum_{e_l \in E} \sum_{w_p \in e_l} \sum_t I(z_p = (t, y))}{\sum_{e_l \in E} |e_l|}. \tag{5.10}$$

Initialization of the latent variable z_p is also important to modelling accuracy as well as inference efficiency. Traditional collapsed Gibbs sampling on standard LDA usually employs simple initialization with uniform topic sampling. In our problem setting, however, the overall score of the review reflects opinions of the user on the scores. It is thus meaningful to include the overall score in the initialization procedure. In particular, each z_p contributes to the overall score y with probability $1/S$, where S is the total number of words in the complete review with multiple snippets. By deliberately omitting w_p, z_{-p}, α and c, we can initialize the probability of $z_p = (t, s)$ by a much simpler estimation below.

$$\begin{aligned}\Pr(z_p = (t, s)|\beta, \gamma, y) \\ &\propto \frac{1}{S}\Pr(y|z_p = (t, s))\Pr(z_p = (t, s)|\beta, \gamma) \\ &+ \frac{S-1}{S}\Pr(z_p = (t, s)|\beta, \gamma).\end{aligned} \tag{5.11}$$

Note that the equation above utilizes the aggregation step over y in the generative model, which randomly picks up a snippet and uses its score as the overall evaluation of the restaurant. Moreover, we hereby emphasize that such initialization aims to improve the convergence rate of the collapsed Gibbs sampling, which does not affect the convergence results.

The complete pseudocodes are available in Algorithm 5.4. The algorithm initializes the latent variable with Equation (5.11) on line 2, such that words in reviews with good overall score are more likely to be assigned to aspect-score pair with higher score. In the iteration beginning with line 3, the algorithm keeps updating the probability distribution for each word and draw samples on the topics of the words. The algorithm also updates the

---

Algorithm 5.4 Inference(words $\{w_1, w_2, \ldots, w_l\}$, *max* number of iterations Q, α, β, γ)

1: Initialize the aspect-score pair assignment based on $\Pr(z_p = (t, s))$ using Equation (5.11).

2: **for** each iteration **do**

3:     **for** each word w_p in the snippets **do**

4:         Update $\Pr\left(z_p = (t, s) \mid z_{-p}, w_p, \alpha, c, \beta, \gamma\right)$ with Equation (5.9).

5:         Update $\Pr\left(y \mid z_p, z_{-p}\right)$ using Equation (5.10).

6:         Draw a sample z_p using Equation (5.8).

7:         Update the statistics $N^{(w_p)}_{-p,ts}, N^{(\cdot)}_{-p,ts}, N^{(\cdot)}_{-p,t\cdot}, N^{(\cdot)}_{-p,\cdot s}, N^{(\cdot)}_{-p,\cdot\cdot}$

8:     **end for**

9:     **if** The model has converged or the number of iteration reaches Q **then**

10:         Return all the probabilities as final results.

11:     **end if**

12: **end for**

statistics used in the update of the probabilities of all the other words. When there is model convergence, i.e., the probabilities do not change any more, or the algorithm reaches the pre-defined maximal iteration number Q, the algorithm terminates and returns the current probabilities.

The computation cost of the inference algorithm depends on the number of aspects, the number of scores and the maximal number of iterations. Since the algorithm updates the probability for every pair of aspect and score over every word, the CPU cost is $O(m(y_{max} - y_{min} + 1)LQ)$, where m is the number of aspects, $y_{max} - y_{min} + 1$ is the number of scores, L is the total number of words in the snippets and Q is the maximal number of iterations. The memory consumption of the algorithm is $O(m(y_{max} - y_{min} + 1)L)$, as the probabilities and results of Gibbs sampling are kept in the memory all the time. Therefore, the inference algorithm is efficient on both computation and memory consumption, and thus applicable on large-scale datasets.

5.3.3 *Summarization*

The summarization step is important in our framework, as it generates the final summary output to users. The output of summarization contains an estimated score $\hat{y}$ and a group of k representative snippets for each dish.

Given the probabilities of each word with respect to an aspect t and a score y, we could calculate an average probability of a dish d_j from restaurant r_i on the aspects and scores, i.e.,

$$\Pr(r_i, d_j, t, y) = \frac{\sum_{e_l \in E_{ij}} \sum_{w_p \in e_l} I(z_p = (t, y))}{\sum_{e_l \in E_{ij}} |e_l|}.$$

The score of the snippet on aspect t is thus calculated as

$$\mathscr{S}(r_i, d_j, t) = \sum_{y=y_{min}}^{y_{max}} y \cdot \Pr(r_i, d_j, t, y).$$

Finally, the average score of d_j from r_i on all aspects is used in the summarization as the final rating on the dish, i.e.,

$$\hat{y} = \frac{\sum_t \mathscr{S}(r_i, d_j, t)}{m}. \tag{5.12}$$

To formulate the problem of representative snippet selection, we design a concrete closeness function on the snippets. This function is based on the probabilities of the snippets over the pairs of aspect and score, which are output by our inference method in Algorithm 5.4. Particularly, given a snippet e_l, the distribution of the snippet on every pair of aspect t and score y is calculated as

$$P_l(t, y) = \frac{\sum_{w_p \in e_l} I(z_p = (t, y))}{|e_l|}.$$

We can thus employ KL divergence over the distributions P_l and P_u on every pair of snippets e_l and e_u in E_{ij}.

Definition 5.7 (KL Divergence on Snippets). Given two snippets e_l and e_u with the distributions on aspects and scores as P_l and P_u, the KL divergence between the snippets is

$$KL(P_l, P_u) = \sum_{(t,y)} P_l(t, y) \log \frac{P_l(t, y)}{P_u(t, y)}.$$

Combining Definitions 5.6 and 5.7, the problem of summarization optimization is equivalent to the soft clustering problem over KL-divergence. We therefore directly adopt the clustering algorithm proposed by Banerjee *et al.* (2005), in which the algorithm employs k-means style strategy to improve the representation closeness as defined in Definition 5.6. As is shown in [Banerjee *et al.* (2005)], the computation cost of each iteration in the soft clustering algorithm is proportional to the number of candidates and the expected size of the representation set.

In Algorithm 5.5, we list the pseudocodes of the summarization method, which calculates the estimated score $\hat{y}$ and finds representative snippets by clustering. The computation cost of the algorithm is usually not significant, especially when compared against the time-consuming latent variable inference procedure.

5.4 Experimental Results

In this section, we conduct extensive experiments on restaurant reviews crawled from online review sites to evaluate the diversity-based and topic model-based approaches.

Algorithm 5.5 Summarization (snippets E_{ij}, dish d_j, restaurant r_i, topics $\{z_p\}$ on all words in E_{ij})

1: Calculate $\Pr(r_i, d_j, t, y)$ for each pair of t and y.
2: Calculate $\mathscr{S}(r_i, d_j, t)$ for each aspect t.
3: Calculate $\hat{y}$ based on Equation 5.12.
4: Calculate aspect-score distribution P_l for each snippet e_l in E_{ij}.
5: Run clustering algorithm over snippets in E_{ij} based on the aspect-score distributions.
6: Return the clustering result $\hat{E}_{ij}$ and the score $\hat{y}$.

5.4.1 *Dataset*

We have two real experimental datasets crawled from the most popular restaurant review websites in English and Chinese, i.e., *Yelp* and *Dianping*. These datasets contain records of restaurant reviews, with attributes on reviewer's id, overall evaluation score and detailed comments in plain text.

Before testing summarization methods on the text review data, we run the following processing first, including (1) converting all English words into lower cases; (2) performing tokenization on English words using well recognized tokenizer[2] and segmentation tool on Chinese words [Kruengkrai *et al.* (2009)]; and (3) removing stop words. The detailed statistics of the datasets are summarized in Table 5.2.

As there are no existing groundtruth annotations on the restaurant reviews, we employ three graduate students as the annotators to independently label the dataset for evaluation purpose. Particularly, we randomly

Table 5.2: Statistics of *Dianping* and *Yelp* Datasets

	Dianping	*Yelp*
# of restaurants	16,984	3817
mean # of reviews per restaurant	71.70	137.43
mean # of words per comment	89.34	25.60
mean # of dishes per restaurant	10.6	14.25
mean # of snippets per dish	23.69	9.64

[2]https://victorio.uit.no/langtech/trunk/tools/alignment-tools/europarl/tokenizer.perl.

select 200 dishes with more than 20 but less than 30 description snippets, in order to ensure that the selected dishes are popular but not difficult for humans to label. Given a snippet extracted from the comments, the annotators firstly label if the snippet is opinionated or non-opinionated. For each opinionated snippet, they further assign a score from 1 to 5 stars as its sentiment level. They also label the opinionated snippets with one of the three topics, including "smell", "taste", and "appearance". Each snippet is labeled by two annotators, and is discussed to make an agreement if the labels from the annotators are not consistent.

5.4.2 *Results of Diversity-based Approach*

This part of the work takes dianping dataset as the processing objects. There are totally 4,781 labeled data, among which 1,599 ones are labeled as non-evaluative snippets, about 33.37%.

Evaluation Measures. We use accuracy to measure the performance of evaluative snippet classification. The accuracy is computed as:

$$Acc = \frac{N_r}{N_a},$$

where N_r refers to the number of the snippets with correct class and N_a refers to the number of all the labeled snippets.

We propose to evaluate the rating prediction from two perspectives: ranking correlation and error. We use Kendall's tau rank correlation [Lapata (2006)] and two other methods for ranking errors. The first one is the Root of the Mean Square Error (RMSE) [Gunawardana and Shani (2009)], a popular method for the prediction task, shown as follows,

$$RMSE = \sqrt{\frac{\sum_i (s_i - v_i)^2}{N_a}},$$

where s_i is the predicted rating by the system over item i and v_i is the true rating. The second one is the Mean Absolute Error (MAE) [Herlocker *et al.* (2004)] shown as follows:

$$MAE = \frac{\sum_i (|s_i - v_i|)}{N_a}.$$

For diversification evaluation, the primary measure to evaluate our system is CPR (Cumulative Proportionality) [Dang and Croft (2012)]. We also report the scores of ERR-IA [Chapelle *et al.* (2009)] (intent-aware expected reciprocal rank), which takes into account both diversity and relevance. In these measures, results are judged on the basis of novelty and diversity.

The value of CPR at K is computed in the following steps. First, a metric for dis-proportionality at K is calculated as follows:

$$DP@K = \sum_{t_i} c_i(v_i - s_i)^2 + \frac{1}{2}n_{NR}^2,$$

where v_i is the number of relevant snippets that the aspect t_i should have, s_i is the number of relevant snippets the systems found, n_{NR} is the number of non-relevant snippets, and if $v_i \geq s_i$, $c_i = 1$, else $c_i = 0$. We also calculate the DP for a perfect set as follows:

$$IdealDP@K = \sum_{t_i} v_i^2 + \frac{1}{2}K^2.$$

Then, our proportionality measure by normalizing the DP score with IdealDP in order to make it comparable across queries is

$$PR@K = 1 - \frac{DP@K}{IdealDP@K}.$$

Finally, based on PR@K, we compute the value of CPR at K as follows:

$$CPR@K = \frac{\sum_{i=1}^{K} PR@i}{K}.$$

ERR-IA is defined as follows:

$$ERR\text{-}IA@K = \sum_{k=1}^{K} \frac{1}{k} \sum_{j=1}^{M} p_j \sum_{i=1}^{k-1} (1 - R_i^j) R_k^j.$$

Assume snippets of a given product have M subtopics. p_j $(1 \leq j \leq M)$ is a probability indicating a user submitting the product related to subtopic j (the distribution of subtopics for a given product), with $\sum_j^M p_j = 1$. R_i^j is the associated value of relevance, where $R_i^j = 0$ for non-relevant and $R_i^j = 1$ for relevant. $ERR\text{-}IA$ not only considers the diversity and novelty, but also considers the position information. The more relevant the previous documents are, the more discounted the other documents are. This property reflects user behavior.

In the experimental reports, larger CPR@K and ERR-IA@K indicate a better diversification.

Results of Snippet Classification. We compared our approach with the supervised approaches in this task. The systems are listed as follows:

- NB: The system is based on Naïve Bayes classifier [McCallum *et al.* (1998)].
- ME: The system is based on ME classifier [Berger *et al.* (1996)]. We used the tool maxent.[3]
- SVM: The system is based on SVM [Vapnik (1995)]. We used the tool SVM^{light}.[4]
- OURS: Our system.

In the NB, ME and SVM systems, we used Chinese segmented words as features in training and testing. We performed 10-fold cross validation to obtain the results. To tune the threshold value of our system, we used 20% of the labeled data as the development set and 80% as the test data. Then, we reported the scores on the test data.

Figure 5.5 shows the evaluation results of snippet classification. From the figure, we found that our approach performed a little worse than the three supervised systems. However, our system is unsupervised while the NB, ME and SVM systems are supervised. Of course, the results of the supervised systems can also be used for the summarization. But we have to label new training data if we want to apply them at new applications.

Results of Rating Prediction. We compared our methods with two baseline systems in this task. The systems are listed as follows:

- Baseline1: We chose the word with the highest TF–IDF value as the modifier in each snippet. The TF–IDF method is commonly used in

[3] http://homepages.inf.ed.ac.uk/lzhang10/maxent.html.
[4] http://svmlight.joachims.org.

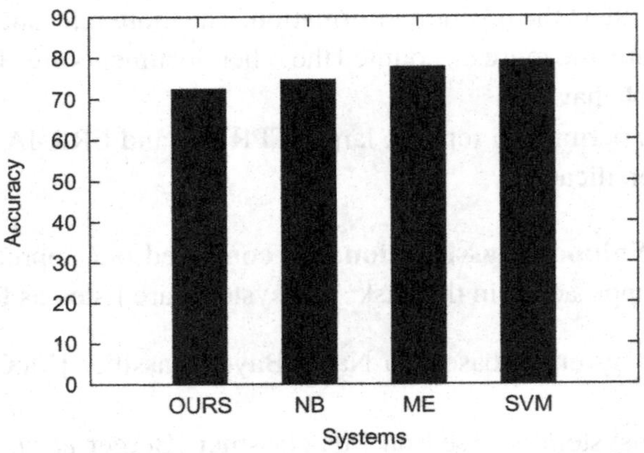

Fig. 5.5: Results of Snippet Classification

information retrieval to choose the informative words [Manning *et al.* (2008)].

- Baseline2: We chose the adjective word which is nearest to the products as the modifier in each snippet. The method of choosing modifiers is similar to the one of [Zhai *et al.* (2011)]. The adjective words can be identified by the Chinese segmentation and POS tagging tool [Kruengkrai *et al.* (2009)].
- DIRECT: The first method introduced in Section 5.2.2.
- AVE: The second method introduced in Section 5.2.2.
- MAX: The third method introduced in Section 5.2.2.

The TF–IDF value [Manning *et al.* (2008)] of word w in snippet *sn* in Baseline1 is computed as follows,

$$TF\text{–}IDF_{w,sn} = (1 + \log tf_{w,sn}) \times \log \frac{N}{df_w}, \tag{5.13}$$

where $tf_{w,sn}$ refers to the frequency of w in *sn*, *N* refers to the number of snippets, and df_w refers to the number of snippets w occurs. In Baseline1 and Baseline2, we used Equation (5.4) to compute the scores of modifiers.

We evaluated the rating prediction in two levels: snippet-based and product-based. In the snippet-based level, we used the scores of snippets as the evaluation units. In the product-based level, we used the scores of products as the evaluation units. The results of rating prediction are shown

Table 5.3: Results of Rating Prediction

	RMSE	MAE	Kendall Tau
(a) Results of Rating Prediction (Snippet-based)			
Baseline1	2.51	1.83	0.38
Baseline2	2.32	1.61	0.50
DIRECT	2.47	1.76	0.45
AVE	**2.08**	**1.40**	**0.62**
MAX	2.16	1.43	**0.62**
(b) Results of Rating Prediction (Product-based)]			
DIRECT	0.50	0.34	0.50
AVE	**0.38**	**0.27**	**0.80**
MAX	0.43	0.29	0.53

in Tables 5.3(a) and 5.3(b). A good prediction should have high Kendall tau value and low RMSE and MAE values. The best performance is marked in bold font for each column in the tables. From Table 5.3, we found that the AVE and MAX systems performed better than the Baseline systems and the DIRECT systems. In Table 5.3(b), the AVE system outperformed the DIRECT and MAX systems in the product-based level. The reason might be that the AVE method considers global information while the DIRECT method only considers local information and the MAX method just uses the maximum rating.

Results of Summarization Diversification. We built the systems based on the Algorithms 5.2 and 5.3. The systems are listed as follows:

- FaDIRECT: We built the system based on Algorithm 5.2 using the output of DIRECT.
- FaAVE: We built the system based on Algorithm 5.2 using the output of AVE.
- FaMAX: We built the system based on Algorithm 5.2 using the output of MAX.
- HiAVE: We built the system based on Algorithm 5.3 using the output of AVE.
- HiMAX: We built the system based on Algorithm 5.3 using the output of MAX.

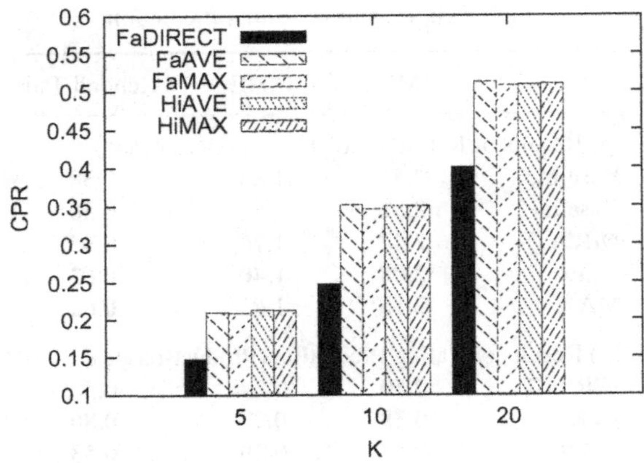

Fig. 5.6: Results of Diversification (CPR)

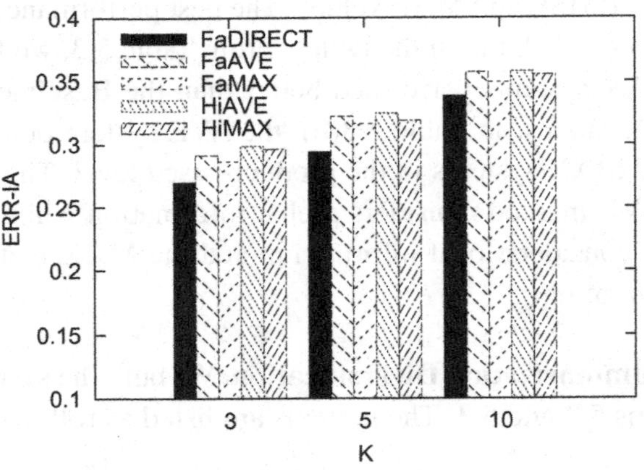

Fig. 5.7: Results of Diversification (ERR-IA)

The FaDIRECT system is used as the baseline system because the DIRECT method uses the direct rating information and Algorithm 5.2 is very close to the standard seat allocation algorithm.

There are two perspectives for diversification evaluation. The first one is based on opinion-aspects and the second one is based on attribute-aspects. The results of opinion-aspects are shown in Figs. 5.6 and 5.7. From the figures, we found that FaAVE and FaMax outperformed FaDIRECT. From

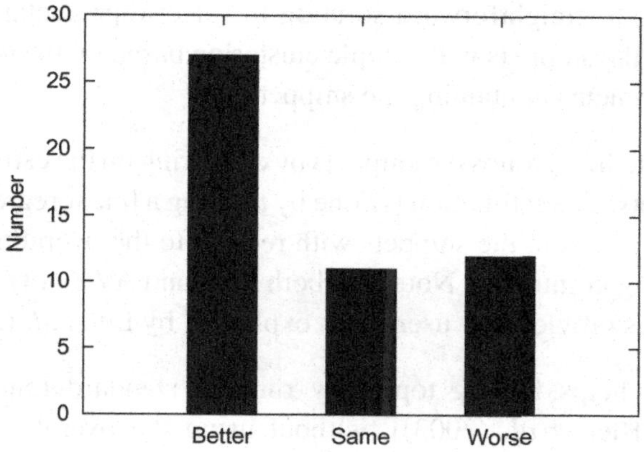

Fig. 5.8: HiAVE vs. FaAVE

the view of opinion-aspects, HiAVE and HiMAX performed similar to FaAVE. These results indicated that better rating predictions can result in better diversification.

Because we did not have a label data to check attribute-aspects, we had to perform human-evaluation. We let the annotators compare 50 product summaries (randomly selected from the results) between HiAVE and FaAVE. The results are shown in Fig. 5.8, where "Better" means HiAVE peforms better, "Worse" means HiAVE is worse, and "Same" means the two systems output the same results. From the figure, we found HiAVE was better than FaAVE. The facts indicate that the hierarchical diversification method is better than flat diversification.

5.4.3 *Results of Topic Model-based Approach*

Datasets. We use both Dianping and Yelp datasets for experiments. We partition each dataset into two parts, with the first (40%) part used for training and second (60%) part used for testing.

Baselines. To evaluate the effectiveness of our bilateral topic model, the inference algorithm and the summarization method, we compare our summarization method based on BTM against state-of-the-art solutions listed as follows:

DIR: This is a straightforward solution to select representative snippets, by grouping the snippets with simple clustering based on the overall scores with the comments containing the snippets.

AVE: This method groups the snippets by clustering on the estimated scores of the snippets. The estimation is done by training a linear regression model on the short grams in the snippets with respect to the overall scores of the corresponding comments. Note that both DIR and AVE only consider the overall scores provided by users as is explained by Lu *et al.* (2009).

LDA: LDA helps finding topics by running standard Latent Dirichlet Allocation [Blei *et al.* (2003)], without using the overall scores of the comments. Given the output of LDA, each snippet is represented as a probability distribution on the identified topics. The clustering algorithm [Banerjee *et al.* (2005)] is then invoked to find the representative snippets.

LRLDA: This is a revised implementation of Wang *et al.* (2011). Wang *et al.* (2011) propose a model combining linear regression and topic modeling on text reviews of products. They assume that each user would initialize a topic distribution θ from a Dirichlet prior to cover different aspects of the product, when writing a new comment. For each word in the comment, their model allows the user to pick up an aspect topic following the distribution θ, and choose a word from the corresponding dictionary of the selected aspect topic. On the other hand, each word is associated with a score under a particular topic [Wang *et al.* (2011)], e.g., *tasty* indicates 5 stars when under the aspect topic *taste*. Finally, the overall score of the snippet is calculated by a weighted sum over the average score on all aspects.

AJM: We directly use the implementation provided by the of Sauper and Barzilay (2013).[5] The dishes of restaurants are treated as aspects in their model, while dishes in our model comprise a high abstract level on top of different attributes, e.g., taste. Their model thus only supports restaurant summarization. To fairly compare AJM with our model, we apply the same pre-processing on the original restaurant text comments and decompose the

[5] http://people.csail.mit.edu/csauper/.

reviews on the restaurants into reviews on dishes. All snippets related to a dish are fed into their algorithm as independent short text documents, with restaurant scores pushed as the above general strategy does.

Without specification, the default parameters of BTM are set as follows, Dirichlet priors as $\alpha = \beta = \gamma = 0.1$, and coin controlling probabilities as $c_0 = 0.4$, $c_1 = c_2 = 0.3$.

Evaluation Measures. To evaluate the effectiveness of snippet pre-processing, we report the accuracy of snippet classification. Specifically, the accuracy is calculated by the following equation:

$$Acc = \frac{N_r}{N_a},$$

in which N_r is the number of returned snippets with opinions, and N_a is the size of the result snippets of the pre-processing step.

Following the diversity task of TREC 2010 Web Track [Clarke *et al.* (2010, 2011)], the primary effectiveness measure to evaluate our system is ERR-IA [Chapelle *et al.* (2009)] (intent-aware expected reciprocal rank), which takes into account both diversity and relevance. We also report the scores of α-nDCG [Clarke *et al.* (2008)] and NRBP [Clarke *et al.* (2009)]. In the measures, results are judged on the basis of novelty (the need to avoid redundancy) and diversity (the need to show aspects).

ERR-IA is defined as follows,

$$ERR\text{-}IA@K = \sum_{k=1}^{K} \frac{1}{k} \sum_{j=1}^{M} p_j \sum_{i=1}^{k-1} (1 - R_i^j) R_k^j. \tag{5.14}$$

Assume snippets of a given dish have M subtopics. p_j $(1 \leq j \leq M)$ is a probability indicating a user submitting the dish related to subtopic j (the distribution of subtopics for a given dish), with $\sum_j^M p_j = 1$. R_i^j is the associated value of relevance, where $R_i^j = 0$ for non-relevant and $R_i^j = 1$ for relevant. $ERR\text{-}IA$ not only considers the diversity and novelty, but also the position information. The more relevant the previous documents are, the more discounted the other documents are. This property reflects user behavior.

α-nDCG is defined as follows,

$$\alpha\text{-}nDCG@K = \sum_{k=1}^{K} \frac{\sum_{j=1}^{M} R_k^j (1-\alpha)^{r_{j,k-1}}}{log_2(1+k)}, \tag{5.15}$$

where $r_{j,k-1} = \sum_{i=1}^{k-1} R_i^j$ and α is a constant that reflects the possibility of assess or error, with $\alpha \in [0, 1]$. R_i^j considers the diversity and $(1-\alpha)^{r_{j,k-1}}$ considers the novelty.

NRBP is a novelty- and rank-biased precision defined as follows,

$$\text{NRBP} = \frac{1-(1-\alpha)\beta}{M} \sum_{k=1}^{\infty} \beta^{k-1} \sum_{j=1}^{M} R_k^j (1-\alpha)^{r_{j,k-1}}, \tag{5.16}$$

where β is a constant probability that the user moves on to read the next results. Different from *ERR-IA* and α-*nDCG*, NRBP is not reported at a particular depth (K), but a true summary measure. Based on existing studies and experience,[6] we set both α and β in evaluation measures α-*nDCG@K* and NRBP to 0.5.

Results on Topic Modeling. In this group of experiments, we aim to verify the usefulness of BTM on finding aspect-related and score-related topics.

We investigate the statistical correlations on the frequencies of the words between topics with respect to different aspects and scores in BTM, as well as the correlations among topics when the same number of topics are trained in standard LDA. We employ Pearson correlation as the underlying measure, which is commonly used in information retrieval and data mining communities. In particular, on the output model of BTM, we merge the topics with respect to each aspect and calculate the average Pearson correlation between word distributions over the aggregated topics, called *outer coefficients*. And for each aspect, we also calculate the average of correlation coefficients among the aspect with different scores, called *inner coefficient*. Similarly, we run the same test by computing outer coefficient and inner coefficient by aggregation over scores. In Tables 5.4(a) and 5.4(b), we report the coefficients found based on the result of BTM on *Yelp* data,

[6]http://trec.nist.gov/data/web/10/ndeval.c.

Table 5.4: Pearson Correlation in BTM and Standard LDA

(a) BTM: pairwise topics under same aspect

	A1	A2	A3	A4	A5	INER
A1	1	−0.21	−0.24	−0.25	−0.31	−0.07
A2	−0.21	1	−0.19	−0.18	−0.26	−0.07
A3	−0.24	−0.19	1	−0.23	−0.30	−0.07
A4	−0.25	−0.18	−0.23	1	−0.27	−0.07
A5	−0.31	−0.26	−0.30	−0.27	1	−0.08

(b) BTM: pairwise topics under same score

	S1	S2	S3	S4	S5	INER
S1	1	−0.20	−0.23	−0.27	−0.26	−0.07
S2	−0.20	1	−0.20	−0.23	−0.24	−0.07
S3	−0.23	−0.20	1	−0.25	−0.26	−0.07
S4	−0.27	−0.23	−0.25	1	−0.30	−0.08
S5	−0.26	−0.24	−0.26	−0.30	1	−0.07

(c) LDA: correlation among topics

	T1	T2	T3	T4	T5
T1	1	−0.93	−0.94	−0.95	−0.93
T2	−0.93	1	−0.94	−0.95	−0.93
T3	−0.94	−0.94	1	−0.96	−0.94
T4	−0.95	−0.95	−0.96	1	−0.95
T5	−0.93	−0.93	−0.94	−0.95	1

where "INER" refers to the inner coefficient. In Table 5.4(c), we also list the average pairwise correlation on standard LDA. From the tables, we find that the outer coefficients are much smaller than the inner coefficients. It means that BTM generates topics with complex and better structure, i.e., topics under same aspect or topics are more compact while other topic pairs are loosely correlated. This is significantly different from the standard LDA, which presents flat and negative correlations between any topic pair. This phenomenon could be used to explain the performance advantage behind BTM, due to its superiority of identifying words for better characterization with respect to customer's opinions on dishes.

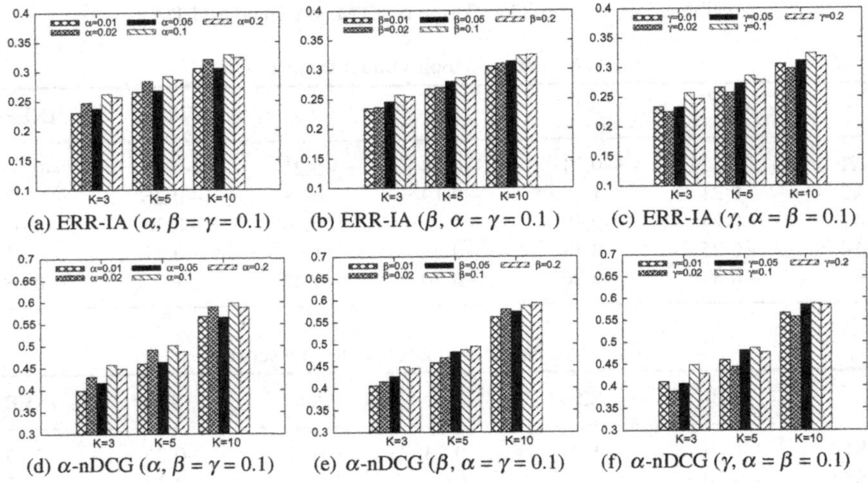

(a) ERR-IA (α, $\beta = \gamma = 0.1$) (b) ERR-IA (β, $\alpha = \gamma = 0.1$) (c) ERR-IA (γ, $\alpha = \beta = 0.1$)

(d) α-nDCG (α, $\beta = \gamma = 0.1$) (e) α-nDCG (β, $\alpha = \gamma = 0.1$) (f) α-nDCG (γ, $\alpha = \beta = 0.1$)

Fig. 5.9: Tuning α, β and γ in BTM on *Yelp*

Results of Summarization. In Fig. 5.9, we test the impact of Dirichlet priors on the *Yelp* dataset for BTM. When testing with a particular evaluation metric, we vary the value of one prior and fix the other two, with default values at $\alpha = 0.1$, $\beta = 0.1$ and $\gamma = 0.1$. The performance of BTM on summarization quality is fairly consistent under two different metrics. It also shows that too small or too large priors could bring negative effects on the summarization goodness. Our default values almost achieve the optimal performance in all settings, which underlies the reason of using these default values in rest of the experiments.

In Fig. 5.10, we tune the aspect number m of our model on *Yelp* dataset. It is straightforward to see that: BTM is unable to distinguish different discussions on the dishes when there are too few aspects, while too many aspects cause BTM to overpartition the topics and lose the key points in the text comments. This intuition is verified in the experiments, when we vary m from 1 to 20. As a quantitative conclusion, BTM performs better when the number of aspect is moderate, i.e., $3 \leq m \leq 5$. In the rest of the section, we use $m = 3$ as the number of aspects.

We then come to the comparisons between all candidate dish comment summarization approaches. Note that the outputs of the first two methods, i.e., DIR and AVE, work in a completely different way as the other four. The

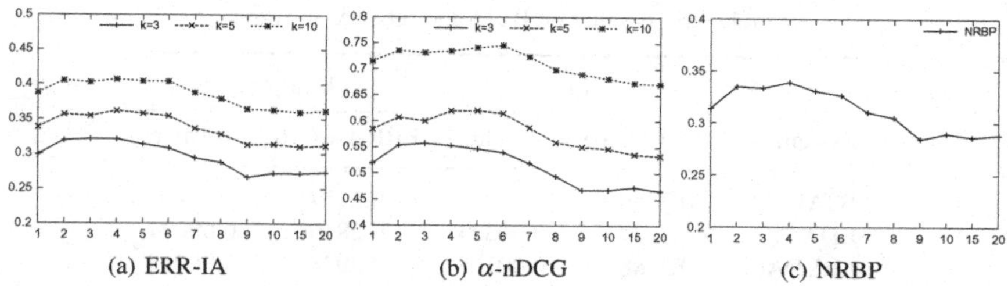

Fig. 5.10: Tuning Aspect Number m in BTM on *Yelp*

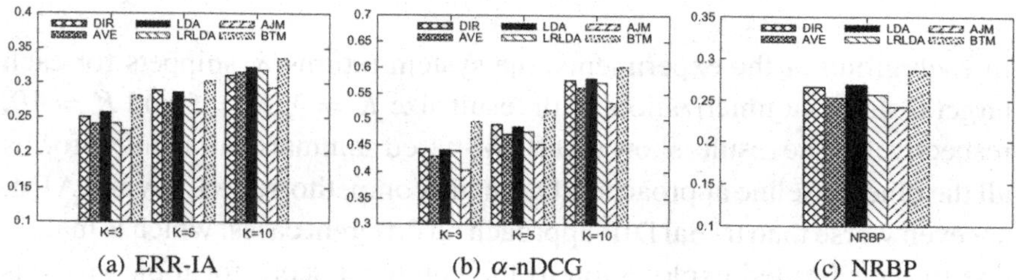

Fig. 5.11: Diversification of Summarization Results on *Yelp*

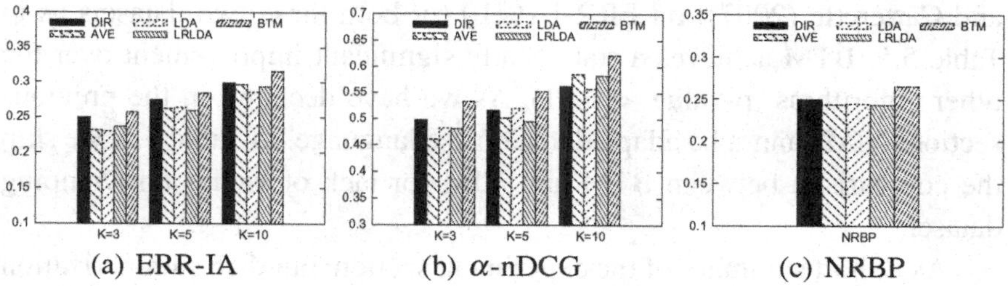

Fig. 5.12: Diversification of Summarization Results on *Dianping*

key difference is that DIR and AVE simply group the snippets, with the final summarization output generated by uniformly picking snippets from every group. The other four methods, instead, output probability vectors on latent topic space for each candidate snippet, and the same clustering algorithm based on KL-divergence (Section 5.3.3) is run to return the specified number of representative snippets.

The overall evaluation results are shown in Figs. 5.11 and 5.12, with ERR-IA measure, α-nDCG measure and NRBP measure, respectively.

Table 5.5: p-value on BTM and other Algorithms

	Yelp		Dianping	
System	ERR-IA@10	p-value	ERR-IA@10	p-value
BTM	0.3359	—	0.3157	—
LDA	0.3227	0.00324	0.2860	0.00074
LRLDA	0.3188	0.00168	0.2938	0.00018
AVE	0.3153	0.00062	0.2966	0.00231
DIR	0.3109	0.00043	0.2987	0.00379

In each group of the experiments, the system returns K snippets for each target dish for summarization, with result size $K = 3$, $K = 5$ and $K = 10$, respectively. The results show that BTM-based summarization outperforms all the other baseline approaches. Our main competitors, LRLDA and AJM, are even worse than trivial DIR approach on different cases, which is mainly due to their limited exploitation to the comment score for topic analysis on dish level. It implies that bilateral topic model is more appropriate on restaurant comment mining. We also run Student's paired t-test [Smucker and Carterette (2007)] on ERR-IA@10 for both these two datasets as in Table 5.5. BTM achieves a statistically significant improvement over the other algorithms (p-value < 0.01). As we have declared in the previous section, AJM cannot be adapted to Chinese language. In Table 5.5, we skip the comparison between BTM and AJM for lack of values on Dianping dataset.

As a short summary of the experiment section, our dish summarization framework with entropy-based unsupervised snippet classification, BTM topic analysis and clustering-based snippet selection method perform significantly better than all state-of-the-art solutions in the literature.

5.5 Conclusion

This chapter studies the problem of review summarization and selection from a large collection of reviews, each of which may refer to several products while giving only one overall evaluation score. Such kind of overall scores cannot cover all the products in a review. Therefore, we propose two approaches to summarize reviews for each of the mentioned product, which includes an evaluation score along with representative snippets. In the first approach, we produce product summarization from both opinion-aspects and attribute-aspects. We extract evaluative snippets and score these snippets. For each product, we select top K snippets proportionally to their distributions on different opinion grades based on the seat-allocation algorithm. We further study a semantic-level snippet selection algorithm by constructing a hierarchical snippet tree so as to ensure selecting a diversified set of snippets. In the second approach, we present a new variant of LDA, which relies on a bilateral topic model with two independent dimensions on the aspects and scores of food, respectively. With an efficient and effective inference algorithm on the new model, this approach performs much better than any of the existing solutions in the literature. While our current methods are designed for the domain of restaurant review text, we believe our proposals are also applicable to other domains with similar structure on comment writing, such as trip reviews. We plan to extend our proposals to support a wider class of products and services in the future. In addition, as comments are changing in both volume and content, designing an algorithm to reflect this kind of dynamics is urgent and it is left for future work.

Chapter 6

Recommendation

Because of the rich information in E-commerce sites, it may take a long time for customers to find what they really need. Consumers have to browse large amounts of unrelated data, and may feel lost in the overloaded information. These problems give birth to the personalized recommendation systems. Recommendation systems provide people with items they are interested based on their experience history. In this chapter, we propose a Comment-based Collaborative Filtering CCF method for recommendation. A topic model is employed on analyzing review text to find hidden topics and the review distribution on topics. Then, we build the rating prediction model to gain the relationship between ratings and topic distributions. We will recommend the products which are top ranked based on these predicated ratings.

6.1 Background

In this section, we introduce the traditional recommendation methods and topic analysis models.

6.1.1 *Traditional Methods*

Recommendation techniques are closely related to some fundamental tasks (e.g., classification, clustering) in machine learning and data mining. Recommendation systems can be regarded as a tool of information filtering, so recommendation algorithms are also known as filtering algorithms. According to the difference among filtering methods, recommendation algorithms can be divided into three categories: content-based filtering, collaborative filtering (CF) and hybrid filtering. The content-based approaches build a profile for each user or item to capture its properties [Blanco-Fernández *et al.* (2008)]. The profile can be described explicit (e.g., user job) and implicit (e.g., user habit). Then, the profiles are used to predict whether users like items. Compared with the content-based approaches, the traditional collaborative filtering approaches make prediction based on the ratings given by similar users, e.g., the scores for items previously viewed or purchased. CF approaches recommend items that have been bought by customers who have the same interests with the user in the past. Hybrid filtering mixes the two methods defined above.

Recently, the rapid development of E-commerce and various online services has brought new challenges for traditional recommendation techniques. For example, most traditional techniques are based on similarity or overlap among existing data, however, there may not exist sufficient historical records for new users to predict their preferences, or users can hold diverse interests, but the similarity-based methods may over-narrow it. Items (e.g., news articles) are changing over time and place. Traditional models that ignore the dynamics of data cannot provide timely and satisfying recommendation. In addition, lots of real-world applications deal with massive datasets with high dimensional features, such that recommendation by traditional techniques is computationally prohibitive.

Moreover, in the age of Web 2.0, customer review comments, which are usually associated with numeric ratings, have become commonly available in many E-commerce sites. These review comments contain abundant information about users' opinions and preferences, which are valuable to any recommendation system. However, in traditional approaches, the review comments are often ignored. The collaborative filtering approaches just consider rating scores while the content-based approaches utilize the predefined description of users and items.

6.1.2 *Topic Analysis*

When talking about computers, we always come up with memory, disks and central processing unit (CPU). When talking about probability, we have probability distributions, standard deviations and conditional independence, because these words appear in corresponding topics with a high probability. An article is usually composed of several topics, and each topic

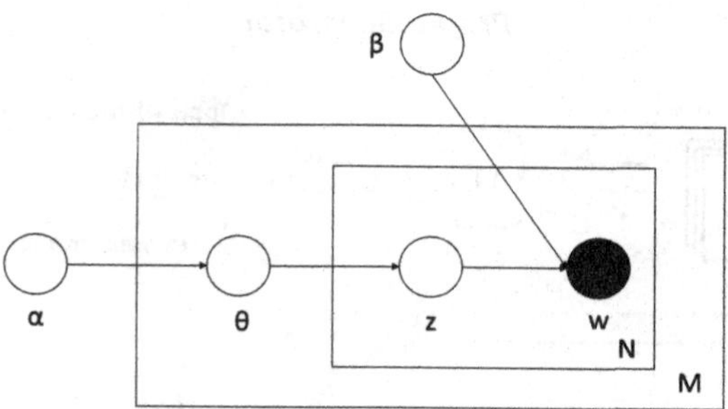

Fig. 6.1: Graphical Model Representation of LDA

can be described with words that are highly related to the topic. This kind of intuitive idea was first proposed as probabilistic latent semantic analysis (PLSA) [Hofmann (1999)].

Similar to PLSA, latent Dirichlet allocation (LDA) is a generative probabilistic model. LDA is a three-level hierarchical Bayesian model that processes collections of discrete data such as text corpora. LDA regards that each document d is composed of a K-dimensional topic distribution θ [Blei *et al.* (2003)]. Meanwhile, words in document d state each of topic k with probability ϕ. It is easily seen that LDA reduces dimensions of the vector space by referencing topic dimension between documents and words. In this work, LDA is used for analyzing aspects hidden in user reviews.

As shown in Fig. 6.1, a document is a sequence of N words and a corpus is a collection of M documents. α and β are two parameters for drawing θ and ϕ separately from the prior probability of the Dirichlet distributions. Here, let z be the topic. From documents to topics and from topics to words, topic distribution θ and word distribution ϕ follow multinomial distributions. Therefore, processing of the corpus and selection of parameters are crucial in the application of LDA to get an ideal result.

6.2 Comment-based Collaborative Filtering Model

The flowchart of our approach to predict ratings is presented in Fig. 6.2. The input to our system is a review corpus and a rating matrix. LDA model is used to uncover hidden aspects in review text and generate user/item profiles with a K-dimensional topic. Combining profiles with rating matrix, we can predict ratings for items that the user has never given reviews based on

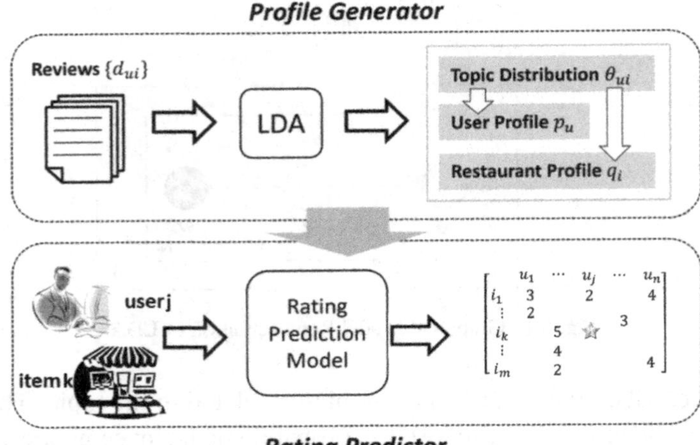

Fig. 6.2: System Flowchart

regression models. As shown in Fig. 6.2, our model consists of two main components: *profile generator* and *rating predictor*.

- **Profile generator** accepts item reviews $\{d_{ui}\}$ as input and outputs user/item profiles, i.e., p_u for user u and q_i for item i.
- **Rating predictor** accepts a pair of user u and item i as input and outputs the rating user u would give to item i.

The two functional components are connected where the output of the profile generator, including topic distributions θ_{ui}, user profile p_u and item profile q_i, are fed into the rating predictor for training regression models and making predictions.

Based on the profiles, we also design a browsing tool to enable efficient access to *representative reviews* of items.

6.2.1 *Profile Generator*

Similar to the method proposed by Koren and Bell (2011), we map users and items to a common latent space $\mathscr{S}$. In this work, we try to discover $\mathscr{S}$ from the review text. The intuition is that reviews, though in the format of unstructured free text, contain information about user preferences and opinions on different aspects of items. These aspects 'hidden' in the review text may well reflect the latent factors that affect the user ratings. To find these hidden aspects and construct the latent space, we apply standard LDA to reviews, as LDA or topic modeling is well recognized as an effective tool for text analysis, extracting prevalent, meaningful and potentially overlapping topics from pure texts. As our experiments show, the topics discovered by LDA are well interpretable and have good correspondence with human-labeled common aspects in restaurant reviews.

Let d_{ui} denote the review of item i by user u. Different from HFT, we treat each d_{ui} as one document. We apply LDA on the review corpus $\{d_{ui}\}$ and discover K topics represented in it. Let θ_{ui} denote the topic distribution of d_{ui} generated by LDA. Define D_u as the set of reviews written by user u, and D_i as the set of reviews written for item i. Each user u (or item i) is associated with a profile p_u (or q_i), which is a vector from $\mathcal{S}$. In our system, $\mathcal{S} = [0, 1]^K$. For a given user u, we define her profile p_u as follows:

$$\begin{aligned} p'_{uj} &= \frac{\sum_i \theta_{uij}}{|D_u|}, \\ p_{uj} &= \frac{p'_{uj}}{\sum_j p'_{uj}}, \; j \in [1, K], \end{aligned} \tag{6.1}$$

where $p_u = (p_{u1}, p_{u2}, \ldots, p_{uK})$, p_{uj} is the distribution on the jth topic for user u, and θ_{uij} is the distribution on the jth topic for review d_{ui}. Similarly, we define profile q_i for item i as:

$$\begin{aligned} q'_{ij} &= \frac{\sum_u \theta_{uij}}{|D_i|}, \\ q_{ij} &= \frac{q'_{ij}}{\sum_j q'_{ij}}, \; j \in [1, K]. \end{aligned} \tag{6.2}$$

In summary, profile p_u/q_i is the normalized average topic distribution over all reviews of a given user u/item i. The notations are summarized in Table 6.1.

6.2.2 *Representation of Samples*

Given a pair of user u and item i, we want to predict the rating $\hat{r}_{ui}$ the user u would give to item i. Recommendations are then made based on $\hat{r}_{ui}$ of items that u has not rated/visited.

Table 6.1: Table of Notations

Symbol	Description
K	# of latent topics, i.e., the dimension of the latent factor space
r_{ui}	rating of item i by user u
$\hat{r}_{ui}$	predicted rating of item i by user u
d_{ui}	review of item i by user u
q_i	profile of item i, $q_i \in [0, 1]^K$
p_u	profile of user u, $p_u \in [0, 1]^K$
θ_{ui}	topic distribution vector for d_{ui}, $\theta_{ui} \in [0, 1]^K$

To predict ratings, we rely on the intuition that hidden topics discovered from review text define the latent factors that affect the ratings. The prediction models (described in Section 6.2.3) learn the relationship between ratings r_{ui} and topic distributions θ_{ui} of d_{ui} on training data and predict the ratings on test data.

Training Samples. As described above, each sample d_{ui} in the training data is represented as a feature vector which has K dimensions (a topic distribution generated by LDA),

$$d_{ui} = [\theta_{ui1}, \ldots, \theta_{uij}, \ldots, \theta_{uiK}]. \tag{6.3}$$

The prediction model is trained on the feature vectors of training data.

Test Samples. When testing, the review comment d_{ui} is not available since user u has not rated item i. Thus, we generate $\hat{d}_{ui}$ based on the profiles p_u and q_i. Each dimensional value of $\hat{d}_{ui}$ is estimated as,

$$\begin{aligned} \theta'_{uij} &= p_{uj} q_{ij}, \\ \hat{\theta}_{uij} &= \frac{\theta'_{uij}}{\sum_j \theta'_{uij}}, \quad j \in [1, K]. \end{aligned} \tag{6.4}$$

Then, $\hat{d}_{ui}$ is represented as,

$$\hat{d}_{ui} = \left[\hat{\theta}_{ui1}, \ldots, \hat{\theta}_{uij}, \ldots, \hat{\theta}_{uiK}\right] \tag{6.5}$$

$\hat{d}_{ui}$ is then fed into the prediction model to predict $\hat{r}_{ui}$.

6.2.3 *Prediction Models*

In our systems, we use different models to learn the relationships between the discovered topics and ratings.

Linear Regression (LR). Linear regression (LR) is a standard regression analysis model used extensively in practical applications. Supposing characteristics and the results are linear, parameters are easier to fit and studied rigorously [Freedman (2009)]. A rating is predicted with multiple linear regression by the following function,

$$\hat{r}_{ui} = W^T d_{ui} + \varepsilon_{ui}, \tag{6.6}$$

where $W = (W_1, \ldots, W_K)$, W_j is the weight of the jth topic and ε_{ui} is an error variable.

Gradient Boosted Regression Tree (GBRT). Gradient boosted regression tree (GBRT) [Friedman (2002)] is a machine learning technique for regression problems, which produces a prediction model in the form of an ensemble of decision trees. Similar to other boosting methods, GBRT combines weak learners into a single strong learner. The target is to learn a model F that predicts values, minimizing the mean squared error to the true values on development sets in each iteration,

- Initialize model with a constant value $F_0(d_{ui})$
- For $m = 1, \ldots, M$
- $F_m(d_{ui}) = F_{m-1}(d_{ui}) + \gamma_m h_m(d_{ui})$, $\gamma_m = \arg\min_\gamma \sum_{(u,i)} L(r_{ui}, F_{m-1}(d_{ui}) + \gamma h_m(d_{ui}))$,

where $h_m(d)$ is a decision tree and $L(r, \bullet)$ is a loss function.

Random Forest (RF). Random forest (RF) [Breiman (2001)] is an ensemble learning method for classification that construct a multitude of decision trees at training time and make decisions by combining the outputs of individual trees. The training algorithm for random forest applies the general idea of bagging to tree learners. The algorithm repeatedly selects a random subset with replacement of the features and fits trees to the training examples,

- For $b = 1, \ldots, B$.
- Sample, with replacement of the features for training examples from the training data; call X_b, Y_b.
- Train a decision tree f_b on X_b, Y_b.

When testing, predictions for a new example $\hat{d}_{ui}$ can be made by averaging the predictions from all the individual trees on $\hat{d}_{ui}$,

$$\hat{r}_{ui} = \frac{1}{B}\sum_{b=1}^{B} f_b(\hat{d}_{ui}). \tag{6.7}$$

6.2.4 *Enhanced Systems*

So far, we have described the CCF systems based on different machine learning techniques. In this part, we enhance the CCF systems by combining a traditional CF approach.

There are many CF methods that have been studied recently. Among them, Bias From Mean (BFM) [Herlocker *et al.* (1999)] is a very efficient method with low computational cost. In BFM, the rating is predicted by,

$$\beta_{ui} = \overline{r_u} + \frac{1}{n}\sum_{v \in Z_i}(r_{vi} - \overline{r_v}), \tag{6.8}$$

where Z_i refers to all the users except u who rated item i and $\overline{r_u}$ is the average value of ratings user u gives.

The prediction models take β_{ui} as an additional feature. For example, the new prediction function for the LR model is,

$$r_{ui} = W^T d_{ui} + W_\beta \beta_{ui} + \varepsilon_{ui}, \tag{6.9}$$

where W_β is the weight for the new feature. All the weights are re-trained on the training data.

6.2.5 *Representative Review Selection*

It is common that an item has hundreds of reviews, which makes it difficult for a user to browse through all of them. Existing review websites either

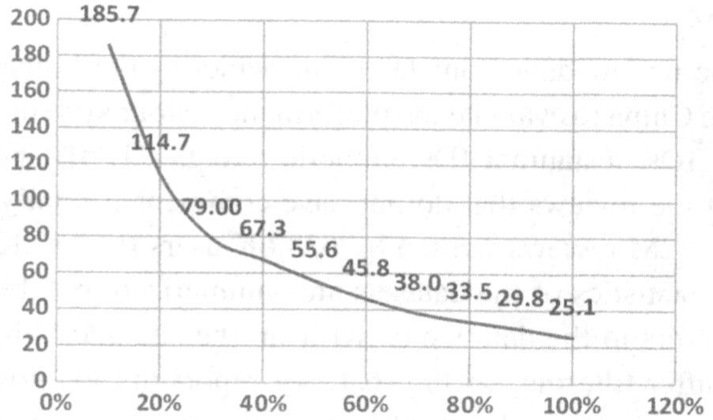

Fig. 6.3: Average Number of Restaurant Reviews

organize reviews by chronological order or provide simple keyword search over reviews. This is, in many cases, not sufficient for users to find useful information out of huge amount of reviews.

When we recommend an item to the user, users would like to get the item's general information and useful reviews of others. According to the survey in our dataset, the restaurant has 1,860 reviews at most and 10% restaurants having most reviews own about 186 reviews on average. The average review numbers appear exponential fall with change of restaurant numbers in Fig. 6.3. In addition to the brief summary, there are 50% restaurants with more than 50 reviews, so it is necessary to select representative reviews.

Our work also provides a new browsing tool that enables efficient access to representative item reviews. A review is considered to be representative if it is "close" enough to the item profile. We measure the closeness between a review r_{ui} and an item i as follows,

$$d(r_{ui}, i) = ||\theta_{ui} - q_i||_2^2. \tag{6.10}$$

Reviews with smallest $d(r_{ui}, i)$ are presented to users as representatives of item i.

6.3 Experimental Results

In this section, we evaluate our systems on a real dataset crawled from online review sites.

6.3.1 *Dataset*

We crawl the review data from *Dianping* which is the biggest restaurant review site in China to evaluate the performance of our system. The reviews contain user IDs, restaurant IDs, numeric ratings ([1, 5]) and comments. We filter out the reviews that do not have comments. Finally, our dataset consists of 3.62M reviews written by 638.6K users for 48.7K restaurants. The detailed statistics of the datasets are summarized in Table 6.2, where "Original" refers to the data we crawl from the site and "Filtered" refers to the data after filtering. In Fig. 6.4, we report the log–log plot of the distributions in terms of the number of users or restaurants with various amount of reviews. The two distributions on users and restaurants follow the power law. We randomly split the whole data set into two sets: 80% as training data and 20% test data.

6.3.2 *Evaluation Metric*

We report the mean absolute error (MAE) of the rating predictor, i.e.,

$$MAE = \frac{1}{N} \sum_{u,i \in T} |\hat{r}_{ui} - r_{ui}|,$$

Table 6.2: Statistics on Dianping Data

	#ofUsers	#ofRestaurants	#ofComments
Original	703.4K	51.5K	4.41M
Filtered	638.6K	48.7K	3.62M

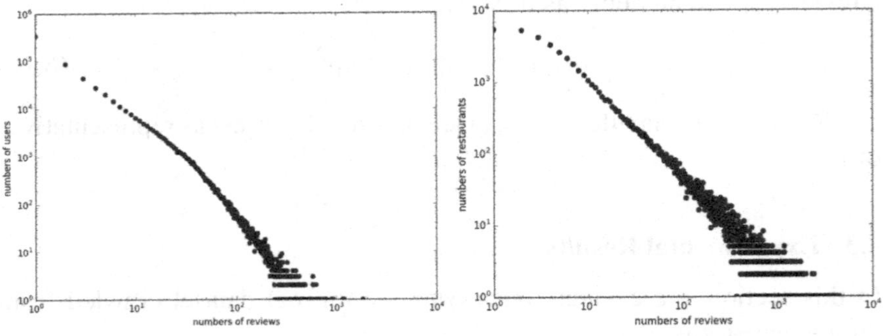

Fig. 6.4: Log–log Plot on Number of Comments and Users/Restaurants

where T is the test set, N is the total number of predicted ratings, $\hat{r}_{ui}$ and r_{ui} are the predicted rating and the user assigned rating scores for user u and item i, respectively.

6.3.3 *Baselines*

In the experiments, we compare our systems with other approaches that are listed as follows:

- BFM: BFM is a CF system based on Bias From Mean described by Herlocker *et al.* (1999).
- SlopeOne: SlopeOne [Lemire and Maclachlan (2005)] is an item-based CF algorithm which is famous for its simplicity and efficiency. Essentially, SlopeOne is a simple form of regression model.
- HFT: As mentioned in the related work, HFT [McAuley and Leskovec (2013)] combines rating dimensions with latent review topics for product recommendation and it is the work most similar to ours. The implementation of HFT is available online.[1]
- CCF-LR and CCF-LR+: CCF-LR refers to the CCF system based on Linear Regression (LR) model and CCF-LR+ refers to the enhanced system that include the CCF-LR system and BFM.
- CCF-GBRT and CCF-GBRT+: CCF-GBRT refers to the CCF system based on GBRT model and CCF-GBRT+ refers to the enhanced system that include the CCF-GBRT system and BFM.
- CCF-RF and CCF-RF+: CCF-RF refers to the CCF system based on Random Forest (RF) model and CCF-RF+ refers to the enhanced system that include the CCF-RF system and BFM.

6.3.4 *Topic Analysis*

We use GibbsLDA[2] to perform topic analysis and set the hyper-parameters $\alpha = 0.2$ and $\beta = 0.1$, and the number of iterations is set to 1000. As for the number of topics, we run the CCF-LR system with different values. The experiment results are shown in Fig. 6.5. From the figure, we find that the system achieves the best score when the number of topics is 6. In

[1] http://cseweb.ucsd.edu/ jmcauley/
[2] http://gibbslda.sourceforge.net

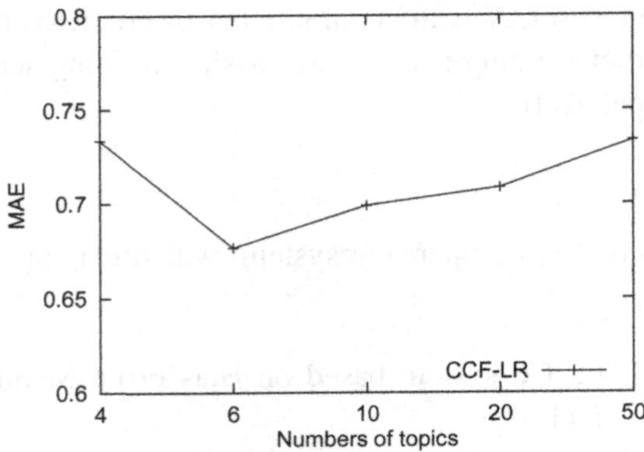

Fig. 6.5: Different Numbers of Topics for LDA

Table 6.3: Main Results of Rating Prediction

Single System	MAE	Enhanced System	MAE
BFM	0.6066		
SlopeOne	0.6885		
HFT	0.6803		
CCF-LR	0.6765	CCF-LR+	0.6004
CCF-GBRT	0.6606	CCF-GBRT+	0.5970
CCF-RF	0.6575	CCF-RF+	0.5938

the following sections, we set the number of topics as 6 for LDA in the experiments.

6.3.5 *Main Results*

Table 6.3 shows the main results of rating prediction on the test data. From the table, we find that BFM performs the best among the baselines. Compared with HFT which also utilizes comments for prediction, our CCF systems achieve better scores. The results also show that the enhanced systems can perform better than the single systems. Among all the systems, CCF-RF+ obtains the highest MAE score. This fact indicates that the information the CCF model learns is different from the information that the traditional CF models learn.

Table 6.4: TOP 10 Topic Words Generated by LDA

Topic1	Topic2	Topic3	Topic4	Topic5	Topic6
好 good	好 good	好 good	菜 dish	服务员 waiter	好 good
味道 taste	味道 taste	味道 taste	味道 taste	好 good	不错 very good
甜 sweet	不错 very good	小 small	不错 very good	菜 dish	环境 environments
蛋糕 cake	好吃 delicious	面 noodle	好 good	店 restaurant	店 restaurant
不错 very good	饭 rice	不错 very good	鱼 fish	团 group	菜 dish
小 small	小 small	汤 soup	辣 spicy	差 bad	味道 taste
奶茶 tea with milk	大 big	店 restaurant	好吃 delicious	态度 manner	感觉 feeling
面包 bread	牛肉 beef	好吃 delicious	香 good smell	东西 goods	朋友 friends
好吃 delicious	鱼 fish	鸡 chicken	虾 shrimp	钱 money	价格 price
茶 tea	锅 hot pots	大 big	大 big	少 few	小 small

6.3.6 *Further Analysis*

In the main experiments, our comment-based systems have shown their efficiency in predicting scores. Here, we investigate the topic words generated by LDA to know how the systems work. The TOP 10 topic words (of 6 topics) are shown in Table 6.4. From the table, we can infer the topics from the words although there are some overlapped words among the topics. The corresponding topics of Topic[1–6] are: Sweets and drinks, Meat and hot pots, Noodles, Vegetable dishes, Services and Environments. We also find that there are some words that are not related to the topics. The prediction systems still have room to improve further. We leave it for future work.

6.4 Conclusion

Our work proposes a CCF approach which utilizes the review comments to predict rating scores. Compared with the traditional CF approaches, our approach makes prediction based on the comments given by similar users rather than the ratings. In our approach, the relationships between users and interdependencies among products are connected via analyzing the review comments. We first apply a topic model to analyze each comment to obtain hidden topics which represent users' opinions or preferences. Then, profiles of users and items are represented by the hidden topics. Finally, we use classifiers to predict rating scores based on the profiles. The systems are further enhanced by combining the traditional CF model.

Chapter 7

Conclusion

As user participation in online activities becomes popular, reviewing provides a convenient way for sharing online experiences. It covers valuable information in user-generated textual comment, which can be used for precise user modeling and rating predication. It has attracted a great deal of effort on text or opinion mining. However, owing to lack of strict monitoring in information publishing, such as product descriptions or comments, the user-generated data introduce abundant of noise. Additionally, in dealing with the information explosion, one of the useful methods is to generate review summarization. However, traditional summarization methods have the disadvantage of one-object assumption, i.e., one piece of review corresponding to one product. It is not generally acceptable. Moreover, current summarization has not considered about latent semantic relationship among aspects. Though review content has been used to extract information for profiling users or products, the semantic level and the numerical level have not been fully exploited.

We study several representative problems related to review analysis in this book, including customer credibility calculation, entity resolution, review set selection, review summarization and recommendation. First, we design to deal with customer credibility calculation for filtering noise and detecting the real evaluation from each customer, which is implemented by analyzing the difference between individual activity and crowd activity. It is a much general problem than spammer detection. Second, we present two general product resolution solutions, one for centralized platform and the other one for distributed platform. Our methods are applicable to non-structured or sparse dataset. Third, we propose to evaluate topK results (reviews or snippets) on latent semantic level besides syntax level. It provides improved results for representative review selection and review summarization. Fourth, we introduce a bilateral topic model to demonstrate the generation of reviews from both aspect dimension and numerical rating dimension. Review summarization is completed by a soft clustering method with the snippet vectors generated on the word distribution to latent topics. Finally, we lay out a content-based collaborative filtering approach for item recommendation. It generates predicated ratings by mining the relationship between the uncovering interests hidden in the review text and the rating matrix.

As a summary, we list the usage among different topics in our book. Credibility analysis in Chapter 2 is a fundamental component for user management; entity resolution in Chapter 3 is designed for item management. These two works can be used to improve the results in other applications, such as review selection in Chapter 4, review summarization in Chapter 5 and recommendation in Chapter 6. For incredible users, we had better filter their reviews for review evaluation and analyze to avoid deviation. Review selection and summarization are useful for review organization with large set of reviews.

In this book, though we have mined the reviews for information organization, recommendation, and user analysis, there still remains a lot of work to do in the future. First, user credibility analysis shall take into account domain information. The same user may have different credibility for different categories. To study such a problem, it is required to analyze user credibility combined with topic model. Then, we need to design a new model to catch the influence of credibility from different topics. Second, until now package recommendation had few related work, especially for restaurant, where a set of dishes may be defined as Goupon. It is urgent to design a new model to find the relationship between these goupons and user interest. Additionally, the solution is also applicable to travel package recommendation.

Bibliography

Ananthakrishna, R., Chaudhuri, S., and Ganti, V. (2002). Eliminating fuzzy duplicates in data warehouses, in *Proc. of VLDB*, pp. 586–597.

Balog, K., Azzopardi, L., and de Rijke, M. (2009). A language modeling framework for expert finding, *Information Processing & Management* **45**, 1, pp. 1–19.

Banerjee, A., Merugu, S., Dhillon, I. S., and Ghosh, J. (2005). Clustering with Bregman divergences, *Journal of Machine Learning Research* **6**, pp. 1705–1749.

Baraglia, R., De Francisci Morales, G., and Lucchese, C. (2010). Document similarity self-join with MapReduce, in *Proc. of ICDM* (IEEE), pp. 731–736.

Bell, R. M. and Koren, Y. (2007). Lessons from the netflix prize challenge, *Sigkdd Explorations* **9**, pp. 75–79, doi:10.1145/1345448.1345465.

Berger, A. L., Pietra, S. A. D., and Pietra, V. J. D. (1996). A maximum entropy approach to natural language processing, *Journal of Computational Linguistics* **22**, 1, pp. 39–71.

Bilenko, M., Basu, S., and Sahami, M. (2005). Adaptive product normalization: using online learning for record linkage in comparison shopping, in *Proc. of ICDM* (IEEE Computer Society), ISBN 0-7695-2278-5, pp. 58–65, http://dblp.uni-trier.de/db/conf/icdm/icdm2005.html#BilenkoBS05.

Bilenko, M. and Mooney, R. J. (2003). Adaptive duplicate detection using learnable string similarity measures, in *Proc. of KDD* (ACM), pp. 39–48.

Blanco-Fernández, Y., Pazos-Arias, J. J., Gil-Solla, A., Ramos-Cabrer, M., López-Nores, M., García-Duque, J., Fernández-Vilas, A., Díaz-Redondo, R. P., and Bermejo-Muñoz, J. (2008). A flexible semantic inference methodology to reason about user preferences in knowledge-based recommender systems, *Knowledge-Based Systems* **21**, 4, pp. 305–320.

Blei, D. M., Ng, A. Y., and Jordan, M. I. (2003). Latent dirichlet allocation, *Journal of Machine Learning Research* **3**, pp. 993–1022.

Breiman, L. (2001). Random forests, *Machine learning* **45**, 1, pp. 5–32.

Brody, S. and Elhadad, N. (2010). An unsupervised aspect-sentiment model for online reviews, in *Proc. of NAACL* (Association for Computational Linguistics), pp. 804–812.

Brown, J. J. and Reingen, P. H. (1987). Social ties and word-of-mouth referral behavior, *Journal of Consumer Research*, **14**, 3, pp. 350–362.

Bunescu, R. C. and Pasca, M. (2006). Using encyclopedic knowledge for named entity disambiguation, in *Proc. of EACL* (The Association for Computer Linguistics), pp. 9–16, http://acl.ldc.upenn.edu/E/E06/E06-1002.pdf.

Carbonell, J. and Goldstein, J. (1998). The use of MMR, diversity-based reranking for reordering documents and producing summaries, in *Proc. of SIGIR* (ACM), pp. 335–336.

Chaiken, S. (1980). Heuristic versus systematic information processing and the use of source versus message cues in persuasion, *Journal of Personality and Social Psychology* **39**, 5, p. 752.

Chang, C. and Lin, C. (2011). LIBSVM: a library for support vector machines, *ACM Transactions on Intelligent Systems and Technology (TIST)* **2**, 3, p. 27.

Chapelle, O., Metlzer, D., Zhang, Y., and Grinspan, P. (2009). Expected reciprocal rank for graded relevance, in *Proc of CIKM* (ACM), pp. 621–630.

Charikar, M. S. (2002). Similarity estimation techniques from rounding algorithms, in *Proc. of STOC* (ACM), pp. 380–388.

Chaudhuri, S., Ganjam, K., Ganti, V., and Motwani, R. (2003). Robust and efficient fuzzy match for online data cleaning, in A. Y. Halevy, Z. G. Ives, and A. Doan (eds.), *Proc. of SIGMOD* (ACM), ISBN 1-58113-634-X, pp. 313–324, http://dblp.uni-trier.de/db/conf/sigmod/sigmod2003.html#ChaudhuriGGM03.

Christina, S., Aria, H., and Regina, B. (2011). Content models with attitude, in *Proc. of ACL*, pp. 350–358.

Clarke, C., Craswell, N., Soboroff, I., and Cormack, G. (2010). Overview of the TREC 2010 web track, in *Proc of TREC*, Vol. 10.

Clarke, C. L., Craswell, N., Soboroff, I., and Ashkan, A. (2011). A comparative analysis of cascade measures for novelty and diversity, in *Proc of WSDM* (ACM), pp. 75–84.

Clarke, C. L., Kolla, M., Cormack, G. V., Vechtomova, O., Ashkan, A., Büttcher, S., and MacKinnon, I. (2008). Novelty and diversity in information retrieval evaluation, in *Proc of SIGIR* (ACM), pp. 659–666.

Clarke, C. L., Kolla, M., and Vechtomova, O. (2009). An effectiveness measure for ambiguous and underspecified queries, in *Advances in Information Retrieval Theory* (Springer), pp. 188–199.

Cucerzan, S. (2007). Large-scale named entity disambiguation based on wikipedia data, in *Prof. of EMNLP-CoNLL* (ACL), pp. 708–716, http://dblp.uni-trier.de/db/conf/emnlp/emnlp2007.html#Cucerzan07.

Danescu-Niculescu-Mizil, C., Kossinets, G., Kleinberg, J., and Lee, L. (2009). How opinions are received by online communities: a case study on amazon.com helpfulness votes, in *Proc. of WWW* (ACM), pp. 141–150.

Dang, V. and Croft, W. B. (2012). Diversity by proportionality: an election-based approach to search result diversification, in *Proc. of SIGIR* (ACM), pp. 65–74.

De Marneffe, M., MacCartney, B., and Manning, C. (2006). Generating typed dependency parses from phrase structure parses, in *Proc. of LREC*, Vol. 6, pp. 449–454.

Dean, J. and Ghemawat, S. (2008). MapReduce: simplified data processing on large clusters, *Communications of the ACM* **51**, 1, pp. 107–113.

Dellarocas, C. (2000). Immunizing online reputation reporting systems against unfair ratings and discriminatory behavior, in *Proc. of EC* (ACM), pp. 150–157.

Deng, H., Lyu, M. R., and King, I. (2009). A generalized co-HITS algorithm and its application to bipartite graphs, in *Proc. of SIGKDD*, pp. 239–248.

Diao, Q., Qiu, M., Wu, C.-Y., Smola, A. J., Jiang, J., and Wang, C. (2014). Jointly modeling aspects, ratings and sentiments for movie recommendation (JMARS), in *Proc. of SIGKDD* (ACM), pp. 193–202.

Ding, X., Liu, B., and Yu, P. (2008). A holistic lexicon-based approach to opinion mining, in *Proc. of WSDM* (ACM), pp. 231–240.

Dong, X., Halevy, A., and Madhavan, J. (2005). Reference reconciliation in complex information spaces, in *Proc. of SIGMOD* (ACM Press, New York, NY, USA), ISBN 1595930604, pp. 85–96, doi:http://dx.doi.org/10.1145/1066157.1066168, http://dx.doi.org/10.1145/1066157.1066168.

Fellegi, I. P. and Sunter, A. B. (1969). A theory for record linkage, *Journal of the American Statistical Association* **64**, 328, pp. 1183–1210.

Forman, C., Ghose, A., and Wiesenfeld, B. (2008). Examining the relationship between reviews and sales: The role of reviewer identity disclosure in electronic markets, *Information Systems Research* **19**, 3, pp. 291–313.

Freedman, D. (2009). *Statistical Models: Theory and Practice* (Cambridge University Press).

Friedman, J. H. (2002). Stochastic gradient boosting, *Computational Statistics & Data Analysis* **38**, 4, pp. 367–378.

Ganesan, K., Zhai, C., and Viegas, E. (2012). Micropinion generation: an unsupervised approach to generating ultra-concise summaries of opinions, in *Proc. of WWW*, pp. 869–878.

Ganu, G., Elhadad, N., and Marian, A. (2009). Beyond the stars: Improving rating predictions using review text content, in *Proc. of WebDB*, pp. 1–6.

Ghose, A. and Ipeirotis, P. G. (2010). Estimating the helpfulness and economic impact of product reviews: Mining text and reviewer characteristics, *Journal of TKDE* **23**, pp. 1498–1512.

Goemans, M. X. and Williamson, D. P. (1995). Improved approximation algorithms for maximum cut and satisfiability problems using semidefinite programming, *Journal of the ACM (JACM)* **42**, 6, pp. 1115–1145.

Gunawardana, A. and Shani, G. (2009). A survey of accuracy evaluation metrics of recommendation tasks, *Journal of Machine Learning Research* **10**, pp. 2935–2962.

Herlocker, J. L., Konstan, J. A., Borchers, A., and Riedl, J. (1999). An algorithmic framework for performing collaborative filtering, in *Proc. of SIGIR* (ACM), pp. 230–237.

Herlocker, J. L., Konstan, J. A., Terveen, L. G., and Riedl, J. T. (2004). Evaluating collaborative filtering recommender systems, *ACM Transactions on Information Systems (TOIS)* **22**, 1, pp. 5–53.

Hofmann, T. (1999). Probabilistic latent semantic analysis, in *Proc. of UAI*, pp. 289–296.

Hong, Y., Lu, J., Yao, J., Zhu, Q., and Zhou, G. (2012). What reviews are satisfactory: novel features for automatic helpfulness voting, in *Proc. of SIGIR* (ACM), pp. 495–504.

Hu, M. and Liu, B. (2004). Mining and summarizing customer reviews, in *Proc. of SIGKDD*, pp. 168–177.

Indyk, P. and Motwani, R. (1998). Approximate nearest neighbors: towards removing the curse of dimensionality, in *Proc. of STOC* (ACM), pp. 604–613.

Jindal, N. and Liu, B. (2008). Opinion spam and analysis, in *Proc. of WSDM*, pp. 219–230.

Jo, Y. and Oh, A. H. (2011). Aspect and sentiment unification model for online review analysis, in *Proc. of WSDM* (ACM), pp. 815–824.

Jurca, R. and Faltings, B. (2003). An incentive compatible reputation mechanism, in *Proc. of E-Commerce*, pp. 285–292.

Jurca, R. and Faltings, B. (2004). Confess: An incentive compatible reputation mechanism for the online hotel booking industry, in *Proc. of E-Commerce*.

Kannan, A., Givoni, I. E., Agrawal, R., and Fuxman, A. (2011). Matching unstructured product offers to structured product specifications, in C. Apte, J. Ghosh, and P. Smyth (eds.), *Proc. of KDD* (ACM), ISBN 978-1-4503-0813-7, pp. 404–412, http://dblp.uni-trier.de/db/conf/kdd/kdd2011.html#KannanGAF11.

Kiefer, T., Volk, P. B., and Lehner, W. (2010). Pairwise element computation with MapReduce, in *Proc. of HPDC* (ACM), pp. 826–833.

Kim, S., Pantel, P., Chklovski, T., and Pennacchiotti, M. (2006). Automatically assessing review helpfulness, in *Proc. of EMNLP*, pp. 423–430.

Kim, Y. and Shim, K. (2012). Parallel top-k similarity join algorithms using MapReduce, in *Proc. of ICDE* (IEEE), pp. 510–521.

Kolb, L., Thor, A., and Rahm, E. (2010). Parallel sorted neighborhood blocking with MapReduce, *arXiv preprint arXiv:1010.3053*.

Kolb, L., Thor, A., and Rahm, E. (2012a). Dedoop: efficient deduplication with hadoop, in *Proc. of VLDB* (VLDB Endowment), pp. 1878–1881.

Kolb, L., Thor, A., and Rahm, E. (2012b). Load balancing for MapReduce-based entity resolution, in *Proc. of ICDE* (IEEE), pp. 618–629.

Kolb, L., Thor, A., and Rahm, E. (2012c). Multi-pass sorted neighborhood blocking with MapReduce, *Computer Science-Research and Development* **27**, 1, pp. 45–63.

Kolb, L., Thor, A., and Rahm, E. (2013). Don't match twice: redundancy-free similarity computation with MapReduce, in *Proc. of the Second Workshop on Data Analytics in the Cloud* (ACM), pp. 1–5.

Koo, T., Carreras, X., and Collins, M. (2008). Simple semi-supervised dependency parsing, in *Proc. of ACL*, pp. 595–603.

Koren, Y. (2010). Collaborative filtering with temporal dynamics, *Communications of the ACM* **53**, 4, pp. 89–97.

Koren, Y. and Bell, R. (2011). Advances in collaborative filtering, in *Recommender Systems Handbook* (Springer), pp. 145–186.

Koren, Y., Bell, R., and Volinsky, C. (2009). Matrix factorization techniques for recommender systems, *Computer* **42**, 8, pp. 30–37.

Kruengkrai, C., Uchimoto, K., Kazama, J., Wang, Y., Torisawa, K., and Isahara, H. (2009). An error-driven word-character hybrid model for joint Chinese word segmentation and POS tagging, in *Proc. of ACL-IJCNLP*, pp. 513–521.

Lapata, M. (2006). Automatic evaluation of information ordering: Kendall's tau, *Computational Linguistics* **32**, 4, pp. 471–484.

Lappas, T., Crovella, M., and Terzi, E. (2012). Selecting a characteristic set of reviews, in *Proc. of SIGKDD* (ACM), pp. 832–840.

Lappas, T. and Gunopulos, D. (2010). Efficient confident search in large review corpora, *Machine Learning and Knowledge Discovery in Databases*, pp. 195–210.

Laureti, P., Moret, L., Zhang, Y.-C., and Yu, Y.-K. (2006). Information filtering via iterative refinement, *EPL (Europhysics Letters)* **75**, 6, p. 1006.

Lee, T., Wang, Z., Wang, H., and won Hwang, S. (2011). Web scale taxonomy cleansing, in *Proc. of VLDB*, Vol. 4, No. 12, pp. 1295–1306, http://dblp.uni-trier.de/db/journals/pvldb/pvldb4.html#LeeWWH11.

Lemire, D. and Maclachlan, A. (2005). Slope one predictors for online rating-based collaborative filtering, in *Proc. of SDM*, Vol. 5, pp. 1–5.

Levenshtein, V. (1966). Binary codes capable of correcting deletions, insertions, and reversals, *Soviet physics doklady* **10**, 8, pp. 707–710.

Li, B., Li, R.-H., King, I., Lyu, M. R., and Yu, J. X. (2014a). A topic-biased user reputation model in rating systems, *Knowledge and Information Systems*, **44**, 581–607, pp. 1–27.

Li, H., Chen, Z., Liu, B., Wei, X., and Shao, J. (2014b). Spotting fake reviews via collective positive-unlabeled learning, in *Proc. of ICDM*, pp. 899–904.

Li, R., Yu, J., Yang, J., and Cheng, H. (2012). Robust reputation-based ranking on bipartite rating networks, in *Proc. of SDM*, **12**, pp. 612–623.

Liu, J., Cao, Y., Lin, C.-Y., Huang, Y., and Zhou, M. (2007). Low-quality product review detection in opinion summarization, in *Proc. of EMNLP-CoNLL*, pp. 334–342.

Liu, Y., Huang, X., An, A., and Yu, X. (2008). Modeling and predicting the helpfulness of online reviews, in *Proc. of ICDM*, pp. 443–452.

Lu, W., Shen, Y., Chen, S., and Ooi, B. C. (2012). Efficient processing of k nearest neighbor joins using MapReduce, in *Proc. of VLDB*, Vol. 5, No. 10, pp. 1016–1027.

Lu, Y., Tsaparas, P., Ntoulas, A., and Polanyi, L. (2010). Exploiting social context for review quality prediction, in *Proc. of WWW*, pp. 691–700.

Lu, Y., Zhai, C., and Sundaresan, N. (2009). Rated aspect summarization of short comments, in *Proc. of WWW* (ACM), pp. 131–140.

Ma, H., Yang, H., Lyu, M. R., and King, I. (2008). Sorec: social recommendation using probabilistic matrix factorization, in *Proc. of CIKM*, pp. 931–940, doi: 10.1145/1458082.1458205.

Manning, C. D., Raghavan, P., and Schütze, H. (2008). *Introduction to Information Retrieval*, Vol. 1 (Cambridge University Press: Cambridge).

McAuley, J. and Leskovec, J. (2013). Hidden factors and hidden topics: understanding rating dimensions with review text, in *Proc. of Recsys* (ACM), pp. 165–172.

McCallum, A., Nigam, K., *et al.* (1998). A comparison of event models for naive bayes text classification, in *Proc. of AAAI*, Vol. 752 (Citeseer), pp. 41–48.

Medo, M. and Wakeling, J. R. (2010). The effect of discrete vs. continuous-valued ratings on reputation and ranking systems, *EPL (Europhysics Letters)*, **91**, p. 48004.

Mei, Q., Ling, X., Wondra, M., Su, H., and Zhai, C. (2007). Topic sentiment mixture: modeling facets and opinions in weblogs, in *Proc. of WWW*, pp. 171–180, doi:10.1145/1242572.1242596.

Meng, X. and Wang, H. (2009). Mining user reviews: from specification to summarization, in *Proc. of ACL-IJCNLP*, pp. 177–180.

Miller, N., Resnick, P., and Zeckhauser, R. (2005). Eliciting informative feedback: The peer-prediction method, *Management Science* **51**, pp. 1359–1373.

Mitchell, T. (1997). *Machine Learning* (McGraw-Hill, Boston).

Mizzaro, S. (2003). Quality control in scholarly publishing: A new proposal, *Journal of the American Society for Information Science and Technology* **54**, 11, pp. 989–1005.

Moghaddam, S. and Ester, M. (2010). Opinion digger: an unsupervised opinion miner from unstructured product reviews, in *Proc. of CIKM*, ISBN 978-1-4503-0099-5, pp. 1825–1828.

Moghaddam, S. and Ester, M. (2012). On the design of LDA models for aspect-based opinion mining, *Proc. of CIKM*.

Monge, A. E., Elkan, C., *et al.* (1996). The field matching problem: Algorithms and applications. in *Proc. of KDD*, pp. 267–270.

Morinaga, S., Yamanishi, K., Tateishi, K., and Fukushima, T. (2002). Mining product reputations on the web, in *Proc. of KDD*, pp. 341–349.

Mukherjee, A., Kumar, A., Liu, B., Wang, J., Hsu, M., Castellanos, M., and Ghosh, R. (2013a). Spotting opinion spammers using behavioral footprints, in *Proc. of SIGKDD* (ACM), pp. 632–640.

Mukherjee, A., Venkataraman, V., Liu, B., and Glance, N. S. (2013b). What yelp fake review filter might be doing? in *Proc. of ICWSM*, pp. 409–418.

Mulpuru, Sucharita (2008). US eCommerce forecast: 2008 to 2012, *Forrester Research*.

Navarro, G. (2001). A guided tour to approximate string matching, *ACM Computing Surveys (CSUR)* **33**, 1, pp. 31–88.

Newcombe, H., Kennedy, J., Axford, S., and James, A. (1959). Automatic linkage of vital records, *Science* **130**, 3381, pp. 954–959.

Nigam, K., Lafferty, J., and McCallum, A. (1999). Using maximum entropy for text classification, in *Proc. of IJCAI*, pp. 61–67.

Pang, B. and Lee, L. (2008). Opinion mining and sentiment analysis, *Foundations and trends in information retrieval* **2**, 1–2, pp. 1–135.

Papaioannou, T. G. and Stamoulis, G. D. (2005). An incentives mechanism promoting truthful feedback in peer-to-peer systems, in *Proc. of CCGRID* **1**, pp. 275–283.

Petrov, S. and McDonald, R. (2012). Overview of the 2012 shared task on parsing the web, in *Notes of the First Workshop on Syntactic Analysis of Non-Canonical Language (SANCL)*.

Popescu, A.-M. and Etzioni, O. (2005). Extracting product features and opinions from reviews. in *Proc. of HLT*, pp. 339–346.

Qiu, G., Liu, B., Bu, J., and Chen, C. (2011). Opinion word expansion and target extraction through double propagation, *Computational linguistics* **37**, 1, pp. 9–27.

Qu, L., Ifrim, G., and Weikum, G. (2010). The bag-of-opinions method for review rating prediction from sparse text patterns, in *Proc. of Coling* (Association for Computational Linguistics), pp. 913–921.

Rajaraman, Anand and Ullman, Jeffrey D and Ullman, Jeffrey David and Ullman, Jeffrey David (2012). *Mining of massive datasets* (Cambridge University Press), **1**.

Ravikumar, P. D. and Cohen, W. W. (2004). A hierarchical graphical model for record linkage, in D. M. Chickering and J. Y. Halpern (eds.), *Proc. of UAI* (AUAI Press), ISBN 0-9749039-0-6, pp. 454–461, http://dblp.uni-trier.de/db/conf/uai/uai2004.html#RavikumarC04.

Sabater, J. and Sierra, C. (2005). Review on computational trust and reputation models, *Artificial Intelligence Review* **24**, 1, pp. 33–60.

Salakhutdinov, R. and Mnih, A. (2007). Probabilistic matrix factorization, in *Proc. of NIPS*, pp. 1257–1264

Salakhutdinov, R. and Mnih, A. (2008). Bayesian probabilistic matrix factorization using Markov Chain Monte Carlo, in *Proc. of ICML*, pp. 880–887, doi: 10.1145/1390156.1390267.

Sarwar, B., Karypis, G., Konstan, J., and Riedl, J. (2001). Item-based collaborative filtering recommendation algorithms, in *Proc. of WWW* (ACM), pp. 285–295.

Sauper, C. and Barzilay, R. (2013). Automatic aggregation by joint modeling of aspects and values, *Journal of Artificial Intelligence Research (JAIR)* **46**, pp. 89–127.

Shimada, K., Tadano, R., and Endo, T. (2011). Multi-aspects review summarization with objective information, *Procedia-Social and Behavioral Sciences* **27**, pp. 140–149.

Smucker, Mark D, Allan, James and Carterette, Ben (2007). A comparison of statistical significance tests for information retrieval evaluation, in *Proc of CIKM*, pp. 623–632.

Sven Ristad, E. and Yianilos, P. N. (1998). Learning string edit distance, *Pattern Analysis and Machine Intelligence, IEEE Transactions on* **20**, 5, pp. 522–532.

Tejada, S., Knoblock, C., and Minton, S. (2002). Learning domain-independent string transformation weights for high accuracy object identification, in *Proc. of SIGKDD* (ACM), pp. 350–359.

Titov, I. and McDonald, R. (2008a). A joint model of text and aspect ratings for sentiment summarization, in *Proc. of ACL* (ACM), pp. 308–316.

Titov, I. and McDonald, R. (2008b). Modeling online reviews with multi-grain topic models, in *Proc. of WWW* (ACM), pp. 111–120.

Toutanova, K., Klein, D., Manning, C. D., and Singer, Y. (2003). Feature-rich part-of-speech tagging with a cyclic dependency network, in *Proc. of HLT-NAACL* (Association for Computational Linguistics), pp. 173–180.

Tsaparas, P., Ntoulas, A., and Terzi, E. (2011). Selecting a comprehensive set of reviews, in *Proc. of SIGKDD* (ACM), pp. 168–176.

Tsur, O. and Rappoport, A. (2009). Revrank: a fully unsupervised algorithm for selecting the most helpful book reviews, in *Proc. of AAAI*, pp. 154–161.

Vapnik, V. (1995). *The Nature of Statistical Learning Theory* (Springer-Verlag, New York).

Vernica, R., Carey, M. J., and Li, C. (2010). Efficient parallel set-similarity joins using MapReduce, in *Proc. of SIGMOD* (ACM), pp. 495–506.

Wang, C. and Blei, D. M. (2011). Collaborative topic modeling for recommending scientific articles, pp. 448–456 doi:10.1145/2020408.2020480.

Wang, H., Lu, Y., and Zhai, C. (2010). Latent aspect rating analysis on review text data: a rating regression approach, in *Proc of KDD*, pp. 783–792.

Wang, H., Lu, Y., and Zhai, C. (2011). Latent aspect rating analysis without aspect keyword supervision, in *Proc. of KDD*, pp. 618–626.

Winkler, W. E. (2002). Methods for record linkage and Bayesian networks, Tech. Rep. Statistical Research Report Series RRS2002/05, U.S. Bureau of the Census, Washington, D.C.

Whang, S. E., Benjelloun, O., and Garcia-Molina, H. (2009). Generic entity resolution with negative rules, *VLDB J.* **18**, 6, pp. 1261–1277, http://dblp.uni-trier.de/db/journals/vldb/vldb18.html#WhangBG09.

Yu, Y.-K., Zhang, Y.-C., Laureti, P., and Moret, L. (2006). Decoding information from noisy, redundant, and intentionally distorted sources, *Physica A: Statistical Mechanics and its Applications* **371**, 2, pp. 732–744.

Zhai, Z., Liu, B., Zhang, L., Xu, H., and Jia, P. (2011). Identifying evaluative sentences in online discussions, in *Proc. of AAAI*.

Zhan, J., Loh, H. T., and Liu, Y. (2009). Gather customer concerns from online product reviews — a text summarization approach, *Expert Systems with Applications* **36**, 2, pp. 2107–2115.

Zhang, H., Yu, H., Xiong, D., and Liu, Q. (2003). Hhmm-based chinese lexical analyzer ictclas, in *Proc. of SIGHAN*, pp. 184–187.

Zhang, J., Cohen, R., and Larson, K. (2008). A trust-based incentive mechanism for e-marketplaces, in *Proc. of TRUST*, pp. 135–161.

Zhang, Z. and Varadarajan, B. (2006). Utility scoring of product reviews, in *Proc. of CIKM*, pp. 51–57.

Zhao, W. X., Jiang, J., Yan, H., and Li, X. (2010). Jointly modeling aspects and opinions with a MaxEnt-LDA hybrid, in *Proc. of EMNLP*, pp. 56–65.

Zhao, Y. and Karypis, G. (2001). Criterion functions for document clustering: Experiments and analysis, *Machine Learning*.

Zhou, Y.-B., Lei, T., and Zhou, T. (2011). A robust ranking algorithm to spamming, *EPL (Europhysics Letters)* **94**, 4, p. 48002.

Zhu, H., Chen, E., Xiong, H., Cao, H., and Tian, J. (2013). Ranking user authority with relevant knowledge categories for expert finding, *World Wide Web*, **17**, 1081–1107, pp. 1–27.

Zhuang, L., Jing, F., and Zhu, X.-Y. (2006). Movie review mining and summarization, in *Proc. of CIKM*, pp. 43–50.

Index